D1524940

The Scarecrow Author Bibliographies

Sir John Betjeman:

A Bibliography of Writings by and about him

by
Margaret L. Stapleton

with an essay by
Ralph J. Mills, Jr.

The Scarecrow Author Bibliographies, No. 21

The Scarecrow Press, Inc.
Metuchen, N.J.   1974

Library of Congress Cataloging in Publication Data

Stapleton, Margaret L
    Sir John Betjeman: a bibliography of writings by
and about him.

    (The Scarecrow author bibliographies, no. 21)
    1. Betjeman, Sir John, 1906-   --Bibliography.
I. Title.
Z8092.34.S73   016.821'9'12   74-14641
ISBN 0-8108-0758-0

FOREWORD

Anyone examining the numerous writings of Sir John Betjeman is impressed by his versatility. Besides the tremendously popular poet there is the well-informed student of Victorian and ecclesiastical architecture; the topographer whose guides to English counties created a new style of guidebook; the essayist and reviewer, the master of a pleasant journalistic style; and the radio and television personality.

Sir John's long list of writings is accompanied by a much shorter gathering of books and articles about him. I have attempted to compile as complete as possible a listing of published works in English by and about him. No effort has been made to survey writings in other languages.

I have examined over ninety percent of the works listed. Where this was impossible I depended on standard bibliographical sources and on the generous help of librarians in other areas. Their courteous response to my inquiries has enabled me to check many items not available in the libraries of Washington and British Columbia.

I must record my gratitude to Mrs. Agatha Kalkanis of the Detroit Public Library and to James Limbacher of the Dearborn Public Library for examining the list of Betjeman recordings.

I am grateful for my freedom to use the excellent collection of Betjemaniana at the University of Victoria Library where Howard Gerwing is in charge of special collections.

For bibliographical sources I am much indebted to Reinhard Schröder for his work, John Betjemans Lyrik (Hamburg: Helmut Buske Verlag, 1972).

Most of all I am obliged to Prof. Ralph J. Mills, Jr. of the Department of English, University of Illinois at Chicago Circle and to the publishers of the magazine Descant for permission to reprint "The Poetry of John Betjeman: An Appreciation, " which originally appeared in Descant (Spring, 1969).

Margaret L. Stapleton
February 1974

CONTENTS

JOHN BETJEMAN'S POETRY:
AN APPRECIATION*

by Ralph J. Mills, Jr.

As his commentators generally observe, John Betjeman is a phenomenon in contemporary English literature, a truly popular poet. The sudden fame won by his <u>Collected Poems</u> (1958), which sold about 100,000 copies, brought him a wide reputation and made him quickly into a public personality. Critics and reviewers have noted that he is the first poet since John Masefield early in this century, and Byron and Tennyson in the last, to command such an audience. Partial explanation for this reputation is not far to seek. Many readers who have had nothing but distaste for the post-Symbolist poetry of Eliot, Pound, Yeats, and Stevens, for the complexities of Auden's ideas, and for the dense, visceral imagery of Dylan Thomas seem to find in Betjeman a poet whom at last they can understand, whose world, though often at the point of disappearing in actuality or only now available through images drawn from memory, they can recognize as the one in which they live or have lived, and whose range of personal feeling touches their own.

Yet, curiously enough, Betjeman's work is also greatly admired by some of the best and most influential poets and critics. W. H. Auden, who in 1947 edited <u>Slick But Not Streamlined,</u> a selection of

---

*Reprinted with permission from <u>Descant</u> (Forth Worth, Tex.) 13 (Spring, 1969), 2-18.

Betjeman's poems and prose pieces designed to intro-
duce him to American readers, remarked in an intro-
ductory essay his jealousy of certain lines by that poet
which he wished he had written himself. Philip Larkin,
reviewing the Collected Poems, said that Betjeman had
succeeded in writing his own kind of verse in the present age and had been completely untouched by the influences of experimental modernist poetry and its ac-
companying body of critical theories. In other words,
Larkin implied, Betjeman could be a poet, and simply
that, in the manner which suited him best and without
regard for literary fashion. For him, Larkin wrote,
"there has been no symbolism, no objective correlative,
no T. S. Eliot or Ezra Pound, no rediscovery of myth
or language as gesture, no Seven Types or Some Versions...." Finally, Edmund Wilson, in a well-known
passage from The Bit Between My Teeth (1965), names
Betjeman, Auden, and Thomas as the three best poets
in England after Eliot.

Certainly it is very rare in our day to see much
accord between distinguished critics and poets on the
one hand and the general public on the other; but the
very complexity of Betjeman's personality and feelings
beneath the skillful though apparently simple surface
of his verse probably unites, in whatever different
kinds or levels of appreciation, the otherwise remote
members of his audience. He is a poet who ardently
loves an England he knew as a child which is pres-
ently vanishing; and he loathes the welfare state of
massive blocks of apartments, phony effects and plas-
tic objects, impersonality and psychoanalysis, where
"every human quality," as he says, "is classified and
explained, so that spontaneous love and heart are disappearing...." Though Betjeman, as he observes of
himself to Kenneth Allsop in the latter's Scan (1965),
is not a hater but "an enthusiastic and probably emotional person," he does admittedly get "white with
anger" over the destruction of what is natural or beautiful and the replacement of it by the sterile, ugly, or
prefabricated. In his famous poem of invective,
"Slough," he calls down ruin upon that place, which
is not just a modern eyesore but an environment

corroding the lives of its inhabitants. The poem begins with a marvelous satirical invocation:

> Come, friendly bombs, and fall on Slough
> It isn't fit for humans now,
> There isn't grass to graze a cow
> Swarm over, Death!
>
> Come, bombs, and blow to smithereens
> Those air-conditioned, bright canteens,
> Tinned fruit, tinned meat, tinned milk, tinned beans
> Tinned minds, tinned breath.

Though he requests punishment for the "man with
double chin/ Who'll always cheat and always win, " a
philandering business executive of some sort, Betjeman
also asks that "the bald young clerks, " victims of the
system who labor for that fat executive's profit, be
spared; they have been warped by their surroundings
and "do not know/ The birdsong from the radio"; un-
aware of the natural world about them, they gather for
leisure in "bogus Tudor bars" to talk of automobiles.
In a later poem, "The Planster's Vision, " Betjeman
adopts the voice and ideas of the modern town-planner
whose utopian notions allow no room for anything that
has tradition and is consecrated by meaningful human
use; churches and cottages both, in his obsessive view,
must go for they are reminders of the past, of birth
and death, the inexorable movement of time, and the
imperfection and impermanence of individual lives:
such sobering realities disturb the artificial harmony
planned for his metropolis of the future:

> Cut down that timber! Bells, too many and strong,
> Pouring their music through the branches bare,
> From moon-white church-towers down the windy air
> Have pealed the centuries out with Evensong.
> Remove those cottages, a huddled throng!
> Too many babies have been born in there,
> Too many coffins, bumping down the stair,
> Carried the old their garden paths along.
>
> I have a Vision of the Future, chum,

    The workers' flats in fields of soya beans
    Tower up like silver pencils, score on score:
  And Surging Millions hear the Challenge come
    From microphones in communal canteens
    "No Right! No Wrong! All's perfect, evermore."

But such Betjeman versions of Orwell's nightmare
state form a limited part of his work and surely do not
account for his popularity at a time when poets in general take the mechanized urban society for a target.
A larger and more compelling, as well as affirmative,
subject in his poetry, and one which has a special ap-
peal for readers who share a middle or upper-middle
class background similar to the poet's (though the ap-
peal is certainly not restricted to them) is English
topography, for in great measure Betjeman is a topographical poet. That term, however, must not be
taken to emphasize the details of region or place in
poetry to the exclusion of more human concerns; as we
shall see, locations are usually the settings for particular human dramas and experiences. In any event,
there is further wide attraction in the fact that his
poetry is literal and descriptive rather than symbolic;
social rather than private; nostalgic--though balanced
by humor and occasional irony, as well as a pervasive
lightness of touch; beautifully and precisely evocative
of place, period, and the moods they generate. And
the manner of his poetry is musically graceful and
various in form. Eliot, Aldous Huxley, and the Sit-
wells are among the 20th century writers Betjeman
has named as influences on his poems; yet the clearest
and strongest line of descent in his writing leads back
to 18th and 19th century poets such as Cowper, Crabbe,
Tennyson, Dowson, Hardy; the Irish poets Tom Moore
and William Allingham; and a host of lesser figures.
Betjeman has, too, a taste for the topographical and
descriptive poetry of forgotten country clergymen, and
he frequently punctuates his prose essays on architecture and English towns with quotations from their
works. Finally, however, the question of influences
must be put aside for there is no doubt that his poetry
assumes its own kind of originality and identity.

When Betjeman writes about other poets (he seems seldom to do so), as in his essay on "Topographical Verse" from Slick But Not Streamlined or his tribute to Eliot in Richard March and Tambimuttu's symposium, he reflects his own poetic preoccupation with the sense and spirit of place. The American reader coming to Betjeman's poetry for the first time need only be cautioned that it is extremely English, and that place-names or other proper names and various details (some of them belonging to the past, to the 19th century or the Edwardian period) may sometimes escape him; but even if he lacks this information, the implications are, as a rule, clear from the poem's context. Then, too, a perusal of some of Betjeman's books of prose, which treat primarily of architecture and topography or are regional guides, and of Derek Stanford's useful study of him should help to illuminate these aspects of the poetry.

To a considerable extent, the nature of Betjeman's imagination, taste, and personality become perceptible to the reader through his moving autobiography in verse, Summoned by Bells (1960). This blank verse poem, divided into nine chapters of varying lengths, covers chronologically different areas and incidents from the poet's life, starting with his early childhood before World War I (he was born in 1906) and carrying through his period of gay living and youthful aestheticism at Oxford which concluded with his failure in Divinity examinations, his departure from the university, and his entrance into "The Opening World," as the last chapter is called, where he took his first job, as a master in a private school. The poem ends there, though certain incidents mentioned in it are also subjects for earlier short poems and the recent piece, "Cricket Master," from High and Low (1967), which describes vividly some of the painful experiences he had as a novice in his school job.

Betjeman grew up in Middlesex, the only child of comfortable middleclass parents; his father managed a family manufacturing firm which he expected his son to continue, but the poet could not find the beauty or

purpose in it his parent did, a matter that led to an
estrangement between them and created a burden of
guilt the poet has always borne.   Betjeman's clumsiness
and lack of physical coordination or skill and his grow-
ing desire to discover a speech for the world as he
saw and responded to it are nicely set forth at the
finish of the poem's second chapter. The boy is in-
stinctively moving in the direction his life will take,
but he is, simultaneously, attempting to live up to the
expectations his father has for him. This passage
concludes in the present, at the time of writing, with
images which stir up a guilt still undiminished:

        Atlantic rollers bursting in my ears,
    And pealing church-bells and the puff of trains,
    The sight of sailing clouds, the smell of grass
    Were always calling out to me for words.
    I caught at them and missed and missed again.
    "Catch hold," my father said, "catch hold like
        this!"
    Trying to teach me how to carpenter,
    "Not that way, boy! When will you ever learn?"--
    I dug the chisel deep into my hand.
    "Shoot!" said my father, helping with my gun
    and aiming at the rabbit--"Quick boy, fire!"
    But I had not released the safety-catch.
    I was a poet. That was why I failed.
    My faith in the chimera brought an end
    To all my father's hopes. In later years,
    Now old and ill, he asked me once again
    To carry on the firm, I still refused.
    And now when I behold, fresh-published, new,
    A further volume of my verse, I see
    His kind grey eyes look woundedly at mine,
    I see his workmen seeking other jobs,
    And that red granite obelisk that marks
    The family grave in Highgate Cemetery
    Points an accusing finger to the sky.

    The detailed recreation of the past in Summoned
by Bells, as well as in briefer poems, is evidence of
an almost Proustian memory in Betjeman, who confirms
this by saying in the poem that "Childhood is measured

out by sounds and smells/ And sights, before the
dark of reason grows." Indeed, his richest imagina-
tive resources seem to lie in the lost worlds of his
childhood and early youth, their emerging interests and
passionate attachments; these are restored and transformed in his poems. But the same past, of course,
harbors the origins of the poet's melancholy, guilt,
sense of evil, fear of pain and death, and apparent
need for a kind of overmastering love; his authentic
religious convictions do not develop, however, until
quite a bit later. Betjeman has remarked at various
times, no doubt somewhat facetiously, that his is a
case of arrested development at about the age of
twelve. While one obviously cannot accept such a judg-
ment at face value (Betjeman was once fired from his
job as novel-reviewer for a newspaper--and he was a
good reviewer--because he was thought by the editor to
be too highbrow!), the elements in life which hold profound significance and value for him--except his ma-
ture Anglican faith--that is to say, his love for poetry
and will to be a poet; his sensitive awareness of landscape; his passion for churches, railways, towns, and
architecture: all those materials on which his writing
thrives initially appealed to him in youth. As he tells
us in the second chapter of Summoned by Bells, the
determination to become a poet arrived with literacy:

>   For myself,
> I knew as soon as I could read and write
> That I must be a poet.

                    *   *   *   *   *

> My first attraction was to tripping lines;
> Internal rhyming, as in Shelley's 'Cloud, '
> Seemed then perfection.   'O'er' and 'ere' and 'e'en'
> Were words I liked to use. My father smiled:
> "And how's our budding bard?   Let what you write
> Be funny, John, and be original. "
> Secretly proud, I showed off merrily.
> But surely as the stars above the twigs
> And deeply fearful as the pealing bells
> And everlasting as the racing surf

Blown back upon itself in Polzeath Bay,
My urge was to encase in rhythm and rhyme
The things I saw and felt (I could not think).

Though the urge was present so early, the achieve-
ment understandably was not; but the as yet unrealized
matter of Betjeman's later poems lay all around him in
his infancy and boyhood:

The gap from feeling to accomplishment!
In Highgate days that gap was yawning wide,
But awe and mystery were everywhere ...

As a boy, he explored every stop and station on the
London tube lines, investigated the "unimagined depths
of glade" in Fitzroy Park, and was terrified by a house
near the cemetery and by the "turrets on [a] chapel for
the dead":

"Dong!" went the distant cemetery bell
And chilled for good the east side of the hill
And all things east of me. But in the west
Were health and sunshine, bumps on Hampstead
      Heath,
Friends, comfort, railways, brandy-balls and
      grass;
And west of westward, somewhere, Cornwall lay.

Betjeman's youthful years are thus filled with an
increasing number and variety of experiences, with
what W. H. Auden calls "sacred beings and sacred
events," that is, objects or creatures, landscapes or
happenings, which arouse in an individual a feeling of
awe and prompt him to immediate recognition and response. Auden says in Making, Knowing, and Judging:
"A sacred being cannot be anticipated; it must be en-
countered. On encounter the imagination has no option
but to respond. All imaginations do not recognize the
same sacred beings or events, but every imagination
responds to those it recognizes in the same way. The
impression made upon the imagination by any sacred
being is of an overwhelming but indefinable importance
--an unchangeable quality, an Identity, as Keats said.

I-am-that-I-am is what every sacred being seems to
say." Later Auden adds a statement that seems to
me peculiarly applicable to the majority of Betjeman's
poems: he remarks: "The impulse to create a work
of art is felt when, in certain persons, the passive
awe provoked by sacred beings or events is transformed
into a desire to express that awe in a rite of worship
or homage, and to be fit homage this rite must be
beautiful. This rite has no magical or idolatrous intention; nothing is expected in return."

While occurrences of a psychological and spiritual
kind in Betjeman's life have impressed themselves
deeply upon his imagination as "sacred events," and so
have become the occasions for poems, probably the
largest number of highly significant encounters have
been associated with specific places. Many of the
poems which take the name of a church or a geograph-
ical location for title--"Saint Cadoc," "Parliament Hill
Fields," "Trebetherick," "Original Sin on the Sussex
Coast," "Devonshire Street W. 1," "Greenaway," "Pershore Station, or a Liverish Journey First Class,"
"Hertfordshire," "Tregardock," and "Uffington," to
draw some examples from Collected Poems and High
and Low--are not simply descriptive pieces (a few of
the titles indicate the fact) but dramatic incidents,
real or imagined, set in those locations.

One of the paradisaical places of Betjeman's childhood was Cornwall, and he has devoted a quantity of
poems, both early and late, to it. In Summoned by
Bells, as we saw in a passage previously quoted, he
gives to Cornwall a sort of symbolic status as the ex-
treme ("west of westward") of that direction opposite
to his private associations of fear and death with the
east; the entire fourth chapter of the poem is, more-
over, occupied with recollection of his summers as a
boy on the Cornish coast. A shorter piece, "Trebetherick," demonstrates not only a remarkable memory
for precise detail in this poet but an ability to elicit
from such exact description a certain emotional reso-
nance, which intensifies gradually throughout the poem
and brings it at last to a moving climax. The opening,

while it depends upon remembrance, maintains a rather
even, objective tone; only a few of the peculiarities of
detail--the "trembling sponges, " "wasps in the tea, "
the "squelch of the bladder-wrack, " the fleas--hint at
the passionate feeling underlying these recollections but
still undisclosed:

> We used to picnic where the thrift
>   Grew deep and tufted to the edge;
> We saw the yellow foam-flakes drift
>   In trembling sponges on the ledge
> Below us, till the wind would lift
>   Them up the cliff and o'er the hedge.
> Sand in the sandwiches, wasps in the tea,
> Sun on our bathing-dresses heavy with the wet,
> Squelch of the bladder-wrack waiting for the sea,
> Fleas round the tamarisk, an early cigarette.

The second stanza continues the description; now,
however, memories of place are shown to be intimately
bound up with inward responses, and these, in this instance, are seemingly rooted in the transition from
innocence to experience, the frightening advent of the
knowledge of evil and death. The first part of the
stanza provides once more particulars of the landscape,
coastguard buildings, a cool wood; but the structure
and movement of the sentence in which these appear
lead directly to the revelation of a place of sinister
associations: "And there the Shade of Evil could/
Stretch out at us from Shilla Mill. " We are not told
why this mill exudes the air of malignity assigned to
it; probably the poet could no more explain it now
than in the past. In any case, it prepares us for the
remainder of the stanza where the experiences that
engender fear are more plain to see:

> Thick with sloe and blackberry, uneven in the light,
> Lonely ran the hedge, the heavy meadow was re-
>   mote,
> The oldest part of Cornwall was the wood as black
>   as night,
> And the pheasant and the rabbit lay torn open at
>   the throat.

In spite of unknown terrors and the first sight
of violent death in the animal kingdom, the poem pro-
ceeds in the two closing stanzas toward a mood of
celebration and prayerful thanksgiving, though not before the magnificent rendering of a storm. These last
stanzas also assume a more personal tone, and their
identical concluding lines are composed of a list of
friends who shared these days of youth with the poet
and are here called by first names:

> Then roller into roller curled
> And thundered down the rocky bay,
> And we were in a water-world
> Of rain and blizzard, sea and spray,
> And one against the other hurled
> We struggled round to Greenaway.
> Blesséd be St. Enodoc, blesséd be the wave,
> Blesséd be the springy turf, we pray, we
> pray to thee,
> Ask for our children all the happy days you
> gave
> To Ralph, Vasey, Alastair, Biddy, John and
> me.

The praise in this final stanza is for the pleasures of
a childhood and youth gone, vanished into the past,
but renewed through memory and imagination, its pains
and imperfections dropped away in time. In theme
the poem is quite close to Dylan Thomas's "Fern Hill,"
but the means of treating it could not be more different. Thomas turns his childhood innocence and joy
into myth, linking Welsh countryside and his uncle and
aunt's farm with the unfallen world of Eden; his language and imagery are dense, elaborate, highly meta-
phorical. By comparison, Betjeman's piece is simple,
transparent. While Thomas aims at making a kind of
separate creation from the complex tissue of interre-
lated metaphors and images, Betjeman's purpose is
to try to capture an area of his experience as faithfully
as possible. In Thomas's poetry place is subsumed in
language, in a symbolic universe; but Betjeman's devo-
tion holds fast to the actuality of location and to precise detail, for his emotions are inextricably bound to

them. Then, too, as he remarked to Kenneth Allsop,
he "would like to see verse become an ordinary medi-
um of communication"--hardly the ideal of a poet as
difficult at Thomas.

It is sometimes thought that because Betjeman's
poetic manner is light he is therefore making light of
the subjects he chooses, especially perhaps because
these subjects seem so unlikely when compared with
the materials of most modern poems; for he may take
the Baker Street Station Buffet of the Metropolitan
Railway as subject, or an undenominational chapel.
Yet readers should not forget how much Betjeman
cares for buildings, for modes of life that belong to
a disappearing world. If he is conservative, he is
certainly not stupid and is well aware that change is
inevitable. What he laments is the death of variety
and individuality in buildings as in human lives; and he
angrily rejects, as we saw in "The Planster's Vision, "
the arrogant assumption that both can be predetermined
and mass-produced. His "Monody on the Death of
Aldersgate Street Station" is a strong, passionate de-
claration of his affection for "the walled-in City of
London, smelly and holy, " which appears doomed to
be torn down in exchange for "new white cliffs" of
modern high-rise apartments and office buildings:

> Snow falls in the buffet of Aldersgate station,
>   Soot hangs in the tunnels in clouds of steam.
> City of London! before the next desecration
>   Let your steepled forest of churches be my
>   theme.
>
> Sunday Silence! with every street a dead street,
>   Alley and courtyard empty and cobbled mews,
> Till "tingle tang" the bell of St. Mildred's
>   Bread Street
>   Summoned the sermon taster to high box pews,
>
> And neighbouring towers and spirelets joined
>   the ringing
>   With answering echoes from heavy commer-
>   cial walls

       *   Till all were drowned as the sailing clouds went
            singing
       On the roaring flood of a twelve-voiced peal
            from Paul's.

As the poem continues, the present falls away and
Betjeman's recollection of former years in London
churches comes to mind. But however happy or
abundant these memories, he is returned to realities
of the moment at the end; and the poet can think now
only with regret of the imminent destruction of the
Aldersgate Street station and how little satisfaction a
changed, rebuilt London will give him:

       Last of the east wall sculpture, a cherub gazes
          On broken arches, rosebay, bracken and dock,
       Where once I heard the roll of the Prayer Book
          phrases
       And the sumptuous tick of the old west gal-
          lery clock.

       Snow falls in the buffet of Aldersgate station,
          Toiling and doomed from Moorgate Street
          puffs the train,
       For us of the steam and the gas-light, the lost
          generation,
       The new white cliffs of the City are built in
          vain.

Plainly, since Betjeman commemorates in his
verse what is passing, his notion of the subjects he
chooses and the poems resulting from them involves
a certain conviction of the preservative powers of his
art. As he observed of himself to Kenneth Allsop, a
deep strain of melancholy runs in his personality which
at least complements if it does not foster the poet's
pessimistic view of contemporary society and its de-
humanizing tendencies. But his poems also spring from
loyalties and affections as fundamental to him as his
melancholy, and the special qualities of his work derive
from the balance and intermingling of these separate
impulses. It is perhaps this emotional climate in Betjeman which makes him react so sharply to the

interpretation of his poetry as ironical. While irony
and satire are occasionally very much in evidence, the
larger gravitation of his poetry is not in that direction.
He has noted that he writes about "ordinary experiences and everyday life, " and in doing so he is sensitive and sympathetic to the anonymous, mundane, or
even slightly seedy aspects of human affairs--an imag-
inative capacity he shares with a writer otherwise as
different as Graham Greene. The little poem "In a
Bath Teashop, " with its impression of dramatizing a
scene witnessed by the author at a neighboring table,
for all of its brevity manages to combine the actuality
of the commonplace with that momentary flare of passion which the poet perceives as transfiguring an or-
dinarily insignificant couple:

> "Let us not speak, for the love we bear one an-
>   other--
>   Let us hold hands and look. "
> She, such a very ordinary little woman;
>   He, such a thumping crook;
> But both, for a moment, little lower than the
>   angels
>   In the teashop's ingle-nook.

What seizes Betjeman's imagination here is the
instant of profound human passion, that moment of
selfless giving in love which redeems a dull or tawdry
existence even though it must rapidly disappear. Simi-
larly, another piece, "Oxford: Sudden Illness at the
Bus-stop, " describes the collapse of an unnamed don's
wife as, dressed for an evening party, she waits for
the bus. In the course of the poem Betjeman ex-
plores the background of her life, the burdens, bore-
dom, and sacrifice of years that lead up to this night
when she is at last physically overwhelmed. Typically,
a few details relating to the town and to university
posts are introduced to support the authentic particu-
larity of the life disclosed, a life as wearisome and
ordinary as that fated to befall the teashop lovers.
Betjeman's compassion is obvious throughout the poem;
here are the concluding stanzas:

What forks since then have been slammed in places?
    What peas turned out from how many a tin?
From plate-glass windows how many faces
    Have watched professors come hobbling in?

Too much, too many! so fetch the doctor,
    This dress has grown such a heavier load
Since Jack was only a Junior Proctor,
    And rents were lower in Rawlinson Road.

Sometimes Betjeman's portraits have a satirical
or pointedly comic intention, but most poems of this
sort seem to appear earlier in his work. One of the
finest and funniest of them is "In Westminster Abbey."
The poem's speaker is a well-to-do woman in the upper half of the social scale who is saying her prayers.
Since the poem was published in a book in 1940, the
reader will not be surprised to find details referring
to World War II and the Germans, but the substance
of the piece is a revelation of class and character in
the speaker. While the revelations are quite humorous, they also give us a person who is selfish, coward-
ly, prejudiced, and whose religion is conceived in
terms appropriate to her financial rather than her
spiritual interests. Beneath her speech she is sadly,
imperfectly human. Her "lady's cry" includes the following stanzas:

Gracious Lord, oh bomb the Germans.
    Spare their women for Thy sake,
And if that is not too easy
    We will pardon Thy Mistake.
But, gracious Lord, whate'er shall be,
Don't let anyone bomb me....

            *   *   *   *   *

Think of what our Nation stands for,
    Books from Boots' and country lanes,
Free speech, free passes, class distinction,
    Democracy and proper drains.
Lord, put beneath Thy special care
One-eighty-nine Cadogan Square.

> Although dear Lord I am a sinner,
>   I have done no major crime;
> Now I'll come to Evening Service
>   Whensoever I have the time.
> So, Lord, reserve for me a crown,
> And do not let my shares go down.

However different their modes of living, the
figures in the last three poems discussed all may be
said to exemplify Betjeman's concern with ordinariness.
Death, too, is ordinary and likewise greatly preoccu-
pies him; his most personal poems, of which we will
speak shortly, often have it for theme. But Betjeman
considers the deaths of others as well as thinking about
his own. The Collected Poems begin with "Death in
Leamington," which once again focuses on lonely,
nameless individuals. The rhythm and lightness of
manner may at first suggest that the poem is not
serious and will end as satire, but that is not the
case:

> She died in the upstairs bedroom
>   By the light of the ev'ning star
> That shone through the plate glass window
>   From over Leamington Spa.

The archaic contraction of "evening" to "ev'ning,"
like similar contractions and various deliberate inver-
sions elsewhere in his work, are conscious poetic
mannerisms on Betjeman's part and must be under-
stood as contributing to the total atmosphere evoked
by the poem. The reader is struck, I believe, by
the feeling that the anonymous life which fades into
death at the poem's beginning was itself archaic,
which is to say, it had long survived in a marginal,
invalid fashion from another era. In the next two
stanzas, though the technique resembles neither of
them, there is a quality of experience which may re-
mind us of Rilke or Neruda, both of whom emphasize
the accumulation of life in "things." The objects
familiar to the deceased woman, previously an integral
part of her living, are suddenly released by her death
and so withdraw, as it were, into their own isolated

being; in doing so they point up the object-like other-
ness into which the body of the woman has retreated
with the departure of her spirit and also the essential
loneliness of the anonymous nurse who unwittingly enters
the sickroom with habitual, forced cheeriness bearing
evening tea and going about her usual preparations for
this daily event before discovering that her patient is
dead. The mechanical character of the nurse's rou-
tine implies a remoteness from all patients (though she
is not so cold and distant as her counterpart in the
later poem "Remorse"), but Betjeman's own compassion pervades the scene and embraces everything--
room and place, victim, objects, and nurse. In the
closing stanzas the nurse's gestures as she leaves the
room create obliquely an air of tender pathos which
joins her briefly to the dead woman. Moving quietly
as if the patient were really still asleep, she performs
a few tasks that not only signify the death but perhaps,
in the manner of their performance, reveal a knowledge of how her own end will come one day:

> And Nurse came in with the tea-things
>   Breast high 'mid the stands and chairs--
> But Nurse was alone with her own little soul,
>   And the things were alone with theirs.
>
> She bolted the big round window,
>   She let the blinds unroll,
> She set a match to the mantle,
>   She covered the fire with coal.
>
> And "Tea!" she said in a tiny voice
>   "Wake up! It's nearly <u>five</u>."
> Oh! Chintzy, chintzy cheeriness,
>   Half dead and half alive!
>
> Do you know that the stucco is peeling?
>   Do you know that the heart will stop?
> From those yellow Italianate arches
>   Do you hear the plaster drop?
>
> Nurse looked at the silent bedstead,
>   At the grey, decaying face,

As the calm of a Leamington ev'ning
Drifted into the place.

She moved the table of bottles
Away from the bed to the wall;
And tiptoeing gently over the stairs
Turned down the gas in the hall.

In the fourth stanza above Betjeman's voice
seems to break with personal urgency into the heart of
the poem, there to announce his own obsession with
time, change, and death; it is not an intrusion that
disconcerts but one that concentrates the interests of
the poem more closely about its thematic center.
That center--man's mortality and the question of the
soul's immortality--is much in evidence in Betjeman's
more personal pieces. Talking with Kenneth Allsop,
he noted of himself and his faith:

> Basically I suppose I am not really a happy
> or cheerful man. It is an effort of will for
> me to believe that good will triumph. I
> am also deeply concerned about personal sur-
> vival. I dread the idea of extinction and
> think about death every day. Unless I am
> overwhelmingly busy I am imagining my end
> and the loss of people I love--I dread that.
>
> My only sustaining belief is that the Chris-
> tian faith is probably true. Why, then,
> should I fear death? Well, if you don't have
> doubts what would faith be? Doubts are the
> test of one's faith.

The darker side of Betjeman's thoughts and emotions are quite evident in some of the poems we have
seen with their attachment to the features of an England associated with his childhood and now being re-
moved in favor of a more impersonal, austere type of
architecture suited to a new highly technological mass-
society. In the remarks quoted above his skepticism
about the triumph of good may perhaps refer to his
firm social pessimism and his fierce antipathy to the

monolithic urban state which the future promises; but
the remainder of his comment is personally revealing
and serves to underscore the themes of fear of death,
longing for immortality, and Christian faith that are
present in some of his finest poems.

The death of others, as one would guess, has
always affected this poet deeply. In "A Child Ill" he
gazes with anguish at one of his own children who is
seriously sick, and in the child's returned look perceives the puzzled questioning by the innocent spirit
of the body's sudden, unexpected frailty:

> Oh, little body, do not die.
> The soul looks out through wide blue eyes
> So questioningly into mine,
> That my tormented soul replies:
>
> "Oh, little body, do not die.
> You hold the soul that talks to me
> Although our conversation be
> As wordless as the windy sky. "

The child's look then awakens memories of the poet's
father on his deathbed, and that sense of loss, and of
a division between father and son that prevented full
understanding, becomes an added torment at the present moment when there is a threat of its recurrence,
only with the poet's role now reversed. Betjeman is
pierced for an instant with the knowledge "that youth-
fulness and age are one"; he recalls once more his
father's gaze and their unfulfilled relationship, then
prays for his son's continued life so that he will not
find this bond severed as well.

A later poem, "Old Friends, " is one of several in which Betjeman commemorates those he has
loved and reflects upon his ties with them. Charac-
teristically, such poems are closely linked with the particulars of place. In this instance the location is
Cornwall. The poem begins with Betjeman arriving at
the familiar coast; the liberating awareness of space
and the special beauties of the evening sky are

described, but in spite of this renewed acquaintance
with a setting of natural loveliness a mood of depres-
sion descends upon him:

> The sky widens to Cornwall. A sense of sea
>   Hangs in the lichenous branches and still there's
>   light.
> The road from its tunnel of blackthorn rises free
>   To a final height,
>
> And over the west is glowing a mackerel sky
>   Whose opal fleece has faded to purple pink.
> In this hour of the late-lit, listening evening, why
>   Do my spirits sink?

The calm hour, the darkening sky are conducive to
recollection, and the poet discovers his mind "full of
the thought of friends" no longer to be seen. Subse-
quent stanzas consist of brief, affectionate portraits of
three dead friends, each viewed in the context of this
spot in Cornwall in such a way that we almost await,
as Betjeman nearly does, their actual appearance, so
much a part of his experience of the durable landscape
are they. The poet continues his drive as night comes
on, but stops the car when he hears the bells of St.
Miniver "from two miles off." Looking up into the
darkened sky with its myriad clusters of stars, he
thinks of the souls of all the dead. The two closing
stanzas move between a recognition of earth, a location in Cornwall where Betjeman still remains, and an
intuition of permanent bonds holding spirit and spirit
together even when separated by the gulf which divides
physical-temporal reality from a transcendent eternal
one. Though he does not know with certainty the character or the nature of their state or whether they pos-
sess sight of the world any longer, the poet feels himself a participant in the invisible dimensions of a vast
spiritual sea and so he wins release from his despon-
dent condition:

> What a host of stars in a wideness still and deep:
> What a host of souls, as a motor-bike whines
>   away

And the silver snake of the estuary curls to sleep
    In Daymer Bay.
Are they one with the Celtic saints and the years
    between?
Can they see the moonlit pools where ribbon-
    weed drifts?
As I reach our hill, I am part of a sea unseen--
The oppression lifts.

The origins of his fear of death and of the in-
comprehensible but nonetheless highly disturbing notion
of eternity are dramatized by Betjeman in his forceful
poem "N. W. 5 and N. 6, " which begins with him watch-
ing the "red cliffs" of "Lissenden Mansions, " buildings
known first in his childhood and now, revisited, bring-
ing to mind images, sounds, smells in a rich confu-
sion from the past that the poet assembles finally in
clearer pictures. The initial recollection is of ob-
serving in a "dark privet hedge where pleasures breed"
the metamorphosis of caterpillar into moth with a boy's
intense curiosity; it is followed by memories of a
child's inevitable questions about dying:

        I see black oak twigs outlined on the sky,
        Red squirrels on the Burdett-Coutts estate.
        I ask my nurse the question "Will I die?"
        As bells from sad St. Anne's ring out so late,
        "And if I do die, will I go to Heaven?"
        Highgate at eventide. Nineteen-eleven.

    We have noted before the astonishing accuracy
of Betjeman's memory, but nowhere in his poetry is
there more explanation for its sharply-etched detail than
in the indelible impressions made upon it by experiences of the sort described here. These are quite
simply unforgettable. His nurse, totally and cruelly
enmeshed in her own anxieties and neuroses, inflicts
them with a vicious, though perhaps partially helpless,
willfulness on the young boy. Like some dreadful
speech in the realms of nightmare which shakes the
sleeper's psyche, she imparts her terror of infinity
and the Divine to him with such conviction that he has

never been able to free himself entirely of its grip on
his mind:

> From that cheap nursery-maid,
> Sadist and puritan as now I see,
> I first learned what it was to be afraid,
> Forcibly fed when sprawled across her knee
> Lock'd into cupboards, left alone all day,
> "World without end. " What fearsome words to
> pray.

> "World without end. " It was not what she'ld do
> That frightened me as much as did her fear
> And guilt at endlessness.   I caught them too,
> Hating to think of sphere succeeding sphere
> Into eternity and God's dread will
> I caught her terror then.   I have it still.

Not surprisingly then, in poems such as "Cottage Hospital" Betjeman can envisage his own death with hal-
lucinatory fascination and horror; his imagined agonies
are all the more vivid and painful here because they
are viewed against the background of nature and childhood which pursue their normal course, innocent of
any knowledge of his suffering and of mortality:

> And say shall I groan in dying,
>   as I twist the sweaty sheet?
> Or gasp for breath uncrying
>   as I feel my senses drown'd
> While the air is swimming with insects
>   and children play in the street?

Yet in any summary account of Betjeman's atti-
tudes his religious faith and hope ultimately outweigh
his fears.   Though his early attraction to Anglicanism
was, by his own admission, aesthetic rather than de-
votional, his writing of the past three decades shows
ample evidence of his firmer beliefs--even though these
are occasionally under attack during spells of anxiety
or dread.   The conclusion of "St. Saviour's, Aberdeen
Park, Highbury, London, N. " offers one of several
instances in which the poet unequivocally articulates

his abiding faith:

> Wonder beyond Time's wonders, that Bread so white
>   and small
> Veiled in golden curtains, too mighty for men to
>   see,
> Is the Power which sends the shadows up this
>   polychrome wall,
> Is God who created the present, the chain-
>   smoking millions and me;
> Beyond the throb of the engines is the throbbing
>   heart of all--
> Christ, at this Highbury altar, I offer myself
> To Thee.

This brief introduction passes over quickly only some of Betjeman's important themes; there are others embodied in excellent poems his readers will discover easily enough for themselves. Great popularity such as his work has acquired may lead certain people to dismiss it as a fashion of the moment, and Betjeman has himself said that he doesn't care about being read fifty years hence (most poets, I think, would prefer to be read and appreciated by their contemporaries); but these are not valid deterrents to his poems which, particular and detailed in the way many of them are and determinedly non-modernist, have the tremendous advantage of being accessible and readable, of achieving a universal significance through their singularity. We also encounter in them the personality of the poet, a man by turns witty, angry, devout, frightened, satirical, tender, and lyrical. In an age of rapid transition and innovation in all the arts, as well as in the other departments of life, Betjeman's poems are quietly but insistently old-fashioned. Unlike many works hailed as great advances, his wear well season after season, authentic expressions of "that spontaneous love and heart" he so rightly admires.

SIR JOHN BETJEMAN: CHRONOLOGY

1906   Born in Highgate, London, August 28, the
                son of Ernest Edward Betjeman, a
                manufacturer, and Mabel Bessie
                (Dawson) Betjeman

1915-1916   Attends Highgate School

1917-1920   Attends Dragon School, Oxford

1920-1925   Attends Marlborough College

1925-1928   Undergraduate Magdalen College, Oxford
                Edits Cherwell, a literary magazine
                Fails divinity examination

1929   Becomes a schoolmaster

1931-1933   Assistant editor of Architectural Review

1931   MOUNT ZION

1933   Marries Penelope Valentine Hester, daugh-
                ter of Field Marshal Lord Chetwode
                GHASTLY GOOD TASTE

1934   Begins editing Shell Guides
                CORNWALL ILLUSTRATED

1934-1935   Film critic on the Evening Standard

1936   DEVON: SHELL GUIDE

1937   CONTINUAL DEW

24

1938	AN OXFORD UNIVERSITY CHEST
1939	ANTIQUARIAN PREJUDICE
1940	OLD LIGHTS FOR NEW CHANCELS
1941-1942	United Kingdom Press Attaché, Dublin, Ireland
1942	VINTAGE LONDON
1943	Serves with the Admiralty Broadcaster for the BBC ENGLISH CITIES AND SMALL TOWNS
1944-1946	With the British Council
1944	ENGLISH, SCOTTISH AND WELSH LANDSCAPE, with Geoffrey Taylor JOHN PIPER
1945	NEW BATS IN OLD BELFRIES
1947	W. S. Auden dedicates The Age of Anxiety to Betjeman SLICK BUT NOT STREAMLINED
1948	SELECTED POEMS MURRAY'S BUCKINGHAMSHIRE ARCHITECTURAL GUIDE
1949	Heinemann Award for Literature for Selected Poems. MURRAY'S BERKSHIRE ARCHITECTURAL GUIDE
1950-1954	Literary Adviser to Time and Tide
1951	THE ENGLISH SCENE SHROPSHIRE (A SHELL GUIDE), with John Piper
1952	FIRST AND LAST LOVES

Book Critic on the <u>Daily Telegraph</u>
Member, Fine Arts Commission (now re-
signed)
Governor of Pusey House, Oxford

1954-1958   Weekly column in the <u>Spectator</u>

1954   <u>POEMS IN THE PORCH</u>
             <u>A FEW LATE CHRYSANTHEMUMS</u>

1955   Foyle Poetry Prize for <u>A Few Late</u>
             <u>Chrysanthemums</u>

1956   <u>THE ENGLISH TOWN IN THE LAST</u>
             <u>HUNDRED YEARS</u>
             Loines Award for Poetry

1957   <u>ENGLISH LOVE POEMS,</u> with Geoffrey
             Taylor
             Poet in Residence at the University of
             Cincinnati
             Hon. Associate, Royal Institute of British
             Architects
             Appears frequently on the BBC

1958   <u>COLLINS GUIDE TO ENGLISH PARISH</u>
             <u>CHURCHES</u>
             <u>JOHN BETJEMAN'S COLLECTED POEMS</u>
             <u>JOHN BETJEMAN</u> [a selection of poems]
             Duff Cooper Memorial Prize for <u>Collected</u>
             <u>Poems</u>

1959   <u>ALTAR AND PEW</u>
             Foyle Poetry Prize for <u>Collected Poems</u>
             Hon. D. Litt., Reading University

1960   <u>A HUNDRED SONNETS</u> by Charles Tenny-
             son Turner, selected in collaboration
             with Sir Charles Tennyson
             <u>GROUND PLAN TO SKYLINE</u>, under pen
             name of Richard Farren
             <u>SUMMONED BY BELLS</u>
             Queen's Gold Medal for Poetry for <u>Col-</u>
             <u>lected Poems</u>

Commander, Order of the British Empire

1962   COLLECTED POEMS [2d ed.] with addi-
        tional poems
        A RING OF BELLS

1963   A WEALTH OF POETRY, with Winifred
        Hindley

1964   ENGLISH CHURCHES, with Basil L. F.
        Clarke
        CORNWALL: A SHELL GUIDE

1965   THE CITY OF LONDON CHURCHES
        Hon. LL. D., Aberdeen University

1966   HIGH AND LOW

1967   SIX BETJEMAN SONGS

1968   Companion of Literature, Royal Society
        of Literature
        COLLINS GUIDE TO ENGLISH PARISH
        CHURCHES

1969   Knight Commander of the British Empire
        Commissioner of the Royal Commission
        on Historical Monuments
        VICTORIAN AND EDWARDIAN LONDON

1970   JOHN BETJEMAN'S COLLECTED POEMS,
        enl. 3rd. ed.
        GHASTLY GOOD TASTE, reprinted with
        the author's comments
        TEN WREN CHURCHES

1971   VICTORIAN AND EDWARDIAN OXFORD
        Hon. Fellow, Royal Institute of British
        Architects

1972   VICTORIAN AND EDWARDIAN BRIGHTON
        LONDON'S HISTORIC RAILWAY STATIONS

Sir John Betjeman

                    A PICTORIAL HISTORY OF ENGLISH
                        ARCHITECTURE
                    Visit of three months to Australia
                    Named Poet Laureate, October 10

1973   Address: 29 Radnor Walk, London
                    SW3 4BP

PART I

THE WRITINGS OF
JOHN BETJEMAN

A. BOOKS OF VERSE

1. John Betjeman's <u>Collected Poems</u>, compiled and with an introduction by the Earl of Birkenhead. London: John Murray, 1958. Contains the poems:

   Death in Leamington
   Hymn
   The 'Varsity Students' Rag
   The City
   An Eighteenth-Century Calvinistic Hymn
   For Nineteenth-Century Burials
   Camberley
   Croydon
   Westgate-on-Sea
   The Wykehamist
   The Arrest of Oscar Wilde at the Cadogan Hotel
   Distant View of a Provincial Town
   Slough
   Clash Went the Billiard Balls
   Love in a Valley
   An Impoverished Irish Peer
   Our Padre
   Exchange of Livings
   Undenominational
   A Hike on the Downs
   Dorset
   Calvinistic Evensong
   Exeter
   Death of King George V
   The Heart of Thomas Hardy
   Cheltenham
   A Shropshire Lad
   Upper Lambourne
   Pot Pourri from a Surrey Garden

Holy Trinity, Sloane Street
On Seeing an Old Poet in the Café Royal
An Incident in the Early Life of Ebenezer Jones,
    Poet, 1828
Trebetherick
Oxford: Sudden Illness at the Bus-stop
Group Life: Letchworth
Bristol and Clifton
Sir John Piers
Myfanwy
Myfanwy at Oxford
Lake District
In Westminster Abbey
Senex
Olney Hymns
On a Portrait of a Deaf Man
Saint Cadoc
Henley-on-Thames
Parliament Hill Fields
A Subaltern's Love-song
Bristol
On an Old-Fashioned Water-Colour of Oxford
A Lincolnshire Tale
St. Barnabas, Oxford
An Archaeological Picnic
May-Day Song for North Oxford
Before Invasion, 1940
Ireland with Emily
Margate, 1940
Invasion Exercise on the Poultry Farm
The Planster's Vision
In a Bath Teashop
Before the Anaesthetic, or A Real Fright
On Hearing the Full Peal of Ten Bells from
    Christ Church, Swindon, Wilts.
Youth and Age on Beaulieu River, Hants
East Anglian Bathe
Sunday Afternoon Service in St. Enodoc Church,
    Cornwall
The Irish Unionist's Farewell to Greta Hellstrom
    in 1922
In Memory of Basil, Marquess of Dufferin and
    Ava

Indoor Games near Newbury
St. Saviour's, Aberdeen Park, Highbury, London
  N.
Beside the Seaside
North Coast Recollections
A Lincolnshire Church
The Town Clerk's Views
Harrow-on-the-Hill
Verses Turned in Aid of a Public Subscription...
Sunday Morning, King's Cambridge
Christmas
The Licorice Fields at Pontefract
Church of England Thoughts...
Essex
Huxley Hall
House of Rest
Middlesex
Seaside Golf
I. M. Walter Ramsden, ob. March 26, 1947, Pem-
  broke College, Oxford
Norfolk
The Metropolitan Railway
Late-Flowering Lust
Sun and Fun
Original Sin on the Sussex Coast
Devonshire Street W. 1
The Cottage Hospital
A Child Ill
Business Girls
Remorse
The Old Liberals
Greenaway
The Olympic Girl
The Dear Old Village
The Village Inn
Station Syren
Hunter Trials
A Literary Discovery
How to Get On in Society
Diary of a Church Mouse
Wantage Bells
Winthrop Mackworth Redivivus
False Security

Eunice
Monody on the Death of Aldersgate Street Station
Thoughts on The Diary of a Nobody
Longfellow's Visit to Venice
Felixstowe, or The Last of Her Order
Pershore Station, or A Liverish Journey First
    Class
Hertfordshire
Lord Cozens Hardy
Variation on a Theme by Newbolt
Inevitable
N. W. 5 & N. 6
From the Great Western
In the Public Gardens

2. _____, compiled and with an introduction by the
Earl of Birkenhead. Boston: Houghton Mifflin,
1959 [c1958].
Contains the same poems as the London edition.

3. Collected Poems, compiled and with an introduction
by the Earl of Birkenhead. London: John Murray,
1959, [c1958].

4. _____. Also a limited edition of 100 autographed
and numbered copies.

5. _____. 2d ed. with additional poems. London:
John Murray, [1962]. (John Murray Paperbacks)

6. John Betjeman's Collected Poems, enl. ed. [3rd ed.],
compiled and with an introduction by the Earl of
Birkenhead. London: John Murray, 1970.
Contains the following additional poems not in
the first edition:

The Sandemanian Meeting-House in Highbury
    Quadrant
City
Suicide on Junction Road Station after Abstention
    from Evening Communion in North London
The Flight from Bootle
Public House Drunk

Blackfriars
South London Sketch, 1944
South London Sketch, 1844
Variations on a Theme by T. W. Rolleston
Preface to High and Low
Cornish Cliffs
Tregardock
By the Ninth Green, St. Enodoc
Winter Seascape
Old Friends
A Bay in Anglesey
A Lament for Moira McCavendish
The Small Towns of Ireland
Ireland's Own
Great Central Railway
Matlock Bath
An Edwardian Sunday, Broomhill, Sheffield
Lines Written to Martyn Skinner
Uffington
Anglo-Catholic Congresses
In Willesden Churchyard
The Commander
Autumn 1964
The Hon. Sec.
Monody on the Death of a Platonist Bank Clerk
Good-bye
Five o'Clock Shadow
A Russell Flint
Perp. Revival i' the North
Agricultural Caress
Narcissus
The Cockney Amorist
Harvest Hymn
Meditation on the A30
Inexpensive Progress
Mortality
Reproof Deserved
Caprice
Cricket Master

7. _____, compiled by the Earl of Birkenhead. En-
larged edition. Introduction by Philip Larkin. Boston: Houghton Mifflin, 1971 [c1970].

Contains the same poems as the 1970 edition
preceding.

8. Continual Dew: A Little Book of Bourgeois Verse.
   London: John Murray, [1937].
   Contains the poems:

   The Arrest of Oscar Wilde at the Cadogan Hotel
   Distant View of a Provincial Town
   Slough
   Public House Drunk
   Suicide on Junction Road Station after Abstention
      from Evening Communion in North London
   When the Great Bell Booms
   Clash Went the Billiard Balls
   Love in a Valley
   An Impoverished Irish Peer
   Our Padre
   Exchange of Livings
   Undenominational
   Tea with the Poets
   A Hike on the Downs
   The Wykehamist at Home
   The Wykehamist
   Dorset
   Calvinistic Evensong
   Exeter
   Death in Leamington
   Hymn
   An Eighteenth-Century Calvinistic Hymn
   For Nineteenth-Century Burials
   The Sandemanian Meeting-House in Highbury
      Quadrant
   Competition
   Tunbridge Wells
   Camberley
   The Outer Suburbs
   The Flight from Bootle
   Croydon
   The Garden City
   Westgate-on-Sea
   [Daily Express] or New King arrives in his
      capital by air ...

9. A Few Late Chrysanthemums: New Poems. London: John Murray, 1954.

Contains the poems:

Sunday Morning, King's Cambridge
Harrow-on-the-Hill
Verses Turned
Christmas
The Licorice Fields at Pontefract
Church of England Thoughts
Essex
Huxley Hall
House of Rest
Middlesex
Seaside Golf
I. M. Dr. Ransden ob. March 26, 1947, Pembroke College, Oxford
Norfolk
Metropolitan Railway
Late-Flowering Lust
Sun and Fun
Original Sin on the Sussex Coast
Devonshire Street W.1
The Cottage Hospital
A Child Ill
Variations on a Theme by T. W. Rolleston
Business Girls
Remorse
The Old Liberals
Clay and Spirit
Greenaway
The Olympic Girl
The Weary Journalist
The Dear Old Village
The Village Inn
Station Syren
Hunter Trials
A Literary Discovery in Surrey, 1869
How to Get On in Society

10. _____, London: John Murray, 1954. Limited to 50 copies.

11. <u>High and Low</u>. London: John Murray, 1966.
    First edition. Limited to 100 copies.

12. _____. [Trade edition]. London: John Murray,
    1966.

13. _____. Boston: Houghton Mifflin, 1967.
    The three editions above contain the following
    poems:

    Preface [in verse]: Murray, you bid my plastic
        pen/
    Cornish Cliffs
    Tregardock
    By the Ninth Green, St. Enodoc
    Winter Seascape
    Old Friends
    A Bay in Anglesey
    A Lament for Moira McCavendish
    The Small Towns of Ireland
    Ireland's Own
    Great Central Railway
    Matlock Bath
    An Edwardian Sunday, Broomhill, Sheffield
    Lines Written to Martyn Skinner
    Uffington
    Anglo-Catholic Congresses
    In Willesden Churchyard
    The Commander
    Autumn 1964
    The Hon. Sec.
    Monody on the Death of a Platonist Bank Clerk
    Good-bye
    Five o'Clock Shadow
    A Russell Flint
    Perp. Revival i' the North
    Agricultural Caress
    Narcissus
    The Cockney Amorist
    Harvest Hymn
    Meditation on the A30
    Inexpensive Progress
    Mortality

Reproof Deserved
Caprice
Cricket Master

14. John Betjeman [A selection of poems].   London:
    Edward Hulton, 1958.   (Pocket Poets)
    Contains the poems:

    Death in Leamington
    Hymn
    The Arrest of Oscar Wilde
    Upper Lambourne
    Undenominational
    Dorset
    Love in a Valley
    Myfanwy
    Spring Morning in North Oxford
    Pot-pourri from a Surrey Garden
    On a Portrait of a Deaf Man
    A Shropshire Lad
    Henley-on-Thames
    East Anglian Bathe
    Bristol
    Norfolk
    Harrow-on-the-Hill
    A Subaltern's Love Song
    Parliament Hill Fields
    Before the Anaesthetic
    House of Rest
    Seaside Golf
    Sun and Fun
    The Licorice Fields at Pontefract
    Business Girls
    Original Sin on the Sussex Coast
    Hunter Trials
    Station Syren
    How to Get on in Society
    Sunday Morning, King's Cambridge
    N. W. 5 and N. 6

15. Mount Zion: or, In Touch with the Infinite.   Lon-
    don: The James Press, 1931.
    Contains the poems:

Death in Leamington
Hymn
The 'Varsity Students' Rag
The City
An Eighteenth-Century Calvinistic Hymn
A Seventeenth-Century Love Lyric
Mother and I
For Nineteenth-Century Burials
Competition
The Sandemanian Meeting-House in Highbury
    Quadrant
Tunbridge Wells
School Song
Camberley
Arts and Crafts
The Outer Suburbs
Croydon
The Flight from Bootle
Westgate-on-Sea
The Wykehamist
The Garden City
St. Aloysius Church, Oxford

16. New Bats in Old Belfries: Poems by John Betje-
    man.   London: John Murray, 1945.
    Contains the poems:

Henley-on-Thames
Parliament Hill Fields
A Subaltern's Love Song
South London Sketch, 1844
South London Sketch, 1944
Bristol
On an Old-Fashioned Water-Colour of Oxford
A Lincolnshire Tale
St. Barnabas, Oxford
The Archaeological Picnic
May-Day Song for North Oxford
Anticipation in Spring
Ireland with Emily
Margate
Invasion Exercise on the Poultry Farm
The Planster's Vision

In a Bath Teashop
Before the Anaesthetic, or, A Real Fright
On Hearing the Full Peal of Ten Bells from
    Christ Church, Swindon, Wilts
Youth and Age on Beaulieu River, Hants
East Anglian Bathe
Sunday Afternoon Service in St. Enodoc Church,
    Cornwall
The Irish Unionist's Farewell to Greta Hellström
    in 1922
In Memory of Basil, Marquess of Dufferin and
    Ava

17. _____. London: John Murray, 1945.
One of a few on special paper, signed.

18. Old Lights for New Chancels: Verses Topographical
and Amatory. London: John Murray, 1940.
Contains the poems:

Cheltenham
A Shropshire Lad
Upper Lambourne
Pot Pourri from a Surrey Garden
Blackfriars
Holy Trinity, Sloane Street MCMVII
On Seeing an Old Poet in the Café Royal
An Incident in the Early Life of Ebenezer Jones,
    Poet, 1828
Trebetherick
Sudden Illness at the Bus-stop
Group Life: Letchworth
Bristol and Clifton
Sir John Piers
Myfanwy
Myfanwy at Oxford
Lake District
In Westminster Abbey
Senex
Olney Hymns
On a Portrait of a Deaf Man
Saint Cadoc

19. Poems in the Porch. [Illustrated by John Piper].
    London: S. P. C. K. , [c1954]. Reprints: 1955,
    1956, 1958.
    Contains the poems:

    Septuagesima
    Diary of a Church Mouse
    Churchyards
    Blame the Vicar
    The Friends of the Cathedral
    Electric Light and Heating

20. A Ring of Bells: Poems of John Betjeman. Intro-
    duced and Selected by Irene Slade. Illustrated by
    Edward Ardizzone. London: John Murray [c1962].

21. _____. Boston: Houghton Mifflin, 1963 [c1962].

22. _____. London: John Murray, 1964. (Paper-
    back)
    These contain the poems:

    Group Life: Letchworth
    False Security
    Croydon
    Indoor Games Near Newbury
    Greenaway
    Parliament Hill Fields
    An Incident in the Early Life of Ebenezer Jones,
        Poet, 1828
    Seaside Golf
    Trebetherick
    East Anglian Bathe
    Beside the Seaside
    Hunter Trials
    The Olympic Girl
    How to Get On in Society
    Pot Pourri from a Surrey Garden
    In the Public Gardens
    A Subaltern's Love-Song
    The Old Liberals
    Lord Cozens Hardy
    Exchange of Livings

Diary of a Church Mouse
Hymn
An Archaeological Picnic
Sunday Morning, King's Cambridge
The Town Clerk's Views
South London Sketch, 1844
Westgate-on-Sea
Margate, 1940
Henley-on-Thames
Wantage Bells
Upper Lambourn [sic]
Hertfordshire
Norfolk
Lake District
Essex
Harrow-on-the-Hill
A Lincolnshire Tale
Distant View of a Provincial Town
Christmas

23. Selected Poems. Chosen, with a preface, by John
    Sparrow. 1st ed. London: John Murray, 1948.
    18 copies, signed.

24. _____. [Trade edition]. London: John Murray,
    1948.

25. _____. London: John Murray, 1952.
    Contains the following poems:

    Parliament Hill Fields
    Before Invasion, 1940
    Bristol
    Dorset
    An Archaeological Picnic
    Upper Lambourne
    Sunday in Ireland
    East Anglian Bathe
    Trebetherick
    Youth and Age on Beaulieu River, Hants
    Henley-on-Thames
    Spring Morning in North Oxford
    Love in a Valley

A Subaltern's Love Song
Pot-Pourri from a Surrey Garden
Indoor Games near Newbury
Croydon
Margate, 1940
St. Saviour's, Aberdeen Park, Highbury,
    London, N.
A Lincolnshire Tale
A Shropshire Lad
An Incident in the Early Life of Ebenezer Jones,
    Poet, 1828
Sir John Piers
Beside the Seaside
In a Bath Teashop
Senex
Myfanwy
Invasion Exercise on the Poultry Farm
Before the Anaesthetic
On a Portrait of a Deaf Man
Death of King George V
Sunday Afternoon Service in St. Enodoc Church,
    Cornwall
North Coast Recollections
Death in Leamington
The Arrest of Oscar Wilde at the Cadogan Hotel
Hymn

26. Sir John Piers, by 'Epsilon' [i. e. , John Betjeman].
    Mullingar, Ireland: The Westmeath Examiner,
    1938? 140 copies. Privately printed.

27. Six Betjeman Songs. Verses by John Betjeman,
    Music by Mervyn Horder. London: Duckworth,
    1967.
    Contains the poems:

    In Westminster Abbey
    How to Get On in Society
    The Church's Restoration
    Westgate-on-Sea
    Caprice
    A Subaltern's Love-Song

28. Slick But Not Streamlined: Poems & Short Pieces,
selected and with an introduction by W. H. Auden.
Garden City: Doubleday, 1947.
Contains the poems:

South London Sketch, 1944
The Arrest of Oscar Wilde at the Cadogan Hotel
In Westminster Abbey
The Flight from Bootle
Parliament Hill Fields
Public House Drunk
Suicide on Junction Road Station after Abstention
    from Evening Communion in North London
Sunday Afternoon Service in St. Enodoc Church,
    Cornwall
Trebetherick
Exeter
In a Bath Teashop
Bristol and Clifton
Youth and Age on Beaulieu River, Hants
Pot Pourri from a Surrey Garden
Love in a Valley
Margate
Westgate-on-Sea
Olney Hymns
East Anglian Bathe
A Lincolnshire Tale
Lake District
Death in Leamington
A Shropshire Lad
Group Life: Letchworth
Sudden Illness at the Bus Stop
May-Day Song for North Oxford
The Wykehamist
Myfanwy at Oxford
On an Old-Fashioned Water-Colour of Oxford
Distant View of a Provincial Town
Before the Anaesthetic, or A Real Fright
In Memory of Basil, Marquess of Dufferin and
    Ava
Senex
Invasion Exercise on the Poultry Farm

Daily Express
Exchange of Livings
On a Portrait of a Deaf Man
Competition
Calvinistic Evensong
The Outer Suburbs
An Impoverished Irish Peer
Sir John Piers
Short Pieces
Provincial Towns
Industrial Towns
North Oxford
A Don Looks at His Fellows
The Morris Works
Ghastly Good Taste
An Apostrophe to One of the Landed Gentry

29. Summoned by Bells. London: John Murray, 1960. Limited edition of 125 signed and numbered copies.

30. ________. [Trade edition.] London: John Murray, 1960.

31. ________. Boston: Houghton Mifflin, [1960].

32. Verses Turned in Aid of a Public Subscription toward the Restoration of the Church of St. Katherine, Chiselhampton, Oxon. Chiselhampton: 1952.

B. PROSE WORKS

33. Antiquarian Prejudice. London: The Hogarth Press, 1939. (Hogarth Sixpenny Pamphlets, No. 3)

34. Cities and Small Towns. London: Collins, 1943. (Britain in Pictures Series)

35. The City of London Churches. [London: Pitkin Pictorials, c1965.] (Pride of Britain Books)

36. English Churches. London: Vista Books, [c1964]. With Basil Fulford Lowther Clarke. "Basil Clarke has been mainly responsible for the text and John Betjeman for the pictures."

37. _____. New York: London House and Maxwell, [1964].

38. English Cities and Small Towns. London: Collins, 1943.

39. _____, in The Englishman's Country, ed. by W. J. Turner. London: Collins, 1945, pp. 101-150.

40. _____, in A Panorama of Rural England, ed. by Walter James Turner. New York: Chantecleer Press, distributed by Hastings House, 1944, pp. 173-220.

41. The English Scene: A Reader's Guide, by John Betjeman. With a Reading List compiled by L. Russell Muirhead. London: Published for the National Book League by the Cambridge University Press, 1951.

47

42. The English Town in the Last Hundred Years.
    Cambridge: The University Press, 1956.   (The
    Rede Lecture, 1956)

43. First and Last Loves. [1st ed.] London: John
    Murray, [1952].

44. _____. [Grey Arrow ed.] London: Arrow
    Books, [1960]. (A Grey Arrow, G53)

45. _____. London: John Murray, 1969. (John
    Murray Paperbacks)

46. Ghastly Good Taste: or, A Depressing Story of
    the Rise and Fall of English Architecture. London:
    Chapman & Hall, 1933.

47. _____. [New ed.] London: Blond, 1970.
    The original text is reprinted with the author's
    current notes.

48. _____. London: Blond, 1970.
    A specially bound, autographed, limited edition
    of 200 copies.

49. _____. New York: St. Martin's Press, [c1971].

50. Ground Plan to Skyline, [by] Richard M. Farren
    [pseud.]. [London: Newman Neame Take Home
    Books, 1960.]

51. John Piper. Harmondsworth, Middlesex: Penguin
    Books, 1944. (The Penguin Modern Painters)

52. _____. [Harmondsworth, Middlesex]: Penguin
    Books, 1948. (The Penguin Modern Painters)

53. London's Historic Railway Stations, [by] John
    Betjeman, photographed by John Gay. [London]:
    John Murray, [1972].

54. An Oxford University Chest. Illustrated in line and
    half-tone by L. Moholy-Nagy [and others]. London:

John Miles, [1938]. Printed at the Chiswick Press.

55. _____. Wakefield: S. R. Publishers, 1970.
Facsimile reprint of first ed., 1938.

56. "Personal Choices," Broadcast. [London: BBC,
20 February 1958]. 13 leaves folio.
One of a few stencil copies with some ms.
revisions.

57. A Pictorial History of English Architecture. London: John Murray, 1972.
Signed, autographed ed. limited to 100 copies.

58. _____. [Trade ed.] London: John Murray,
[1972].

59. _____. New York: Macmillan, 1972.

60. Ten Wren Churches. Illustrated by R. Beer.
London: Editions Electo, 1970.
Limited edition of 100 copies in folder.

61. Vintage London. London: William Collins, 1942.

C. WORKS EDITED BY JOHN BETJEMAN

62. Altar and Pew: Church of England Verses. London: Edward Hulton, [1959].

63. An American's Guide to English Parish Churches, Including the Isle of Man. New York: McDowell, Obolensky, [1959, c1958].

64. Collins Guide to English Parish Churches, Including the Isle of Man. London: Collins, 1958.

65. _____. [Rev. ed.] London: Collins, [1959].

66. Collins Pocket Guide to English Parish Churches. London: Collins, 1968.
     Edited and revised adaptation of Collins Guide to English Parish Churches published in 1958.

67. Cornwall: A Shell Guide. London: Faber and Faber, c1964.

68. Cornwall Illustrated in a Series of Views. London: The Architectural Press, 1934.

69. _____. London: The Architectural Press, 1935. First published June 1934. Second edition April, 1935. (On cover, Shell Guides).

70. Devon: Shell Guide. London: The Architectural Press, [1936].

71. _____. [A reissue]. London: Faber & Faber, [1939].

72. _____, compiled by Brian Watson. New ed.

London: Faber and Faber, 1955.
Originally written by John Betjeman.

73. English Love Poems, chosen by John Betjeman and
Geoffrey Taylor. London: Faber and Faber, [1957].
Contains two poems by Betjeman:

In a Bath Teashop
The Archaeological Picnic

74. _____. [A reduced photographic reprint of the
edition of 1957.] London: Faber & Faber, 1964.

75. English, Scottish and Welsh Landscape, 1700-c1860
(with Geoffrey Taylor). London: Frederick Muller,
1944. (New Excursions into English Poetry)

76. A Hundred Sonnets by Charles Tennyson Turner,
selected and with an introduction by John Betjeman
and Sir Charles Tennyson. London: Hart-Davis,
1960.

77. Murray's Berkshire Architectural Guide (with John
Piper). London: John Murray, [1949].

78. Murray's Buckinghamshire Architectural Guide (with
John Piper). London: John Murray, [1948].

79. Shell Guides. [Illustrated Guides to the counties of
England.] (General editor: John Betjeman). London: Architectural Press, 1934-1964.
In 1937-38 published by B. T. Batsford, and
from 1939 onwards by Faber and Faber.

80. Shropshire (with John Piper). London: Faber and
Faber, [1951]. (A Shell Guide)

81. Victorian and Edwardian Brighton from Old Photographs, [by] John Betjeman and J. S. Gray. London: B. T. Batsford, [1972].

82. Victorian and Edwardian London from Old Photographs: Introduction and commentaries by John

Betjeman. London: B. T. Batsford, [1969].

83. _____. New York: Viking Press, [1969]. (A Studio Book)

84. Victorian and Edwardian Oxford from Old Photographs, [by] John Betjeman and David Vaisey. London: Batsford, 1971.

85. A Wealth of Poetry, selected for the young in heart by Winifred Hindley with the assistance of John Betjeman. [Oxford]: Blackwell, [c1963]. Includes three poems by Betjeman:

    Wantage Bells
    Business Girls
    Christmas

D. CONTRIBUTIONS TO BOOKS

86. "An Architectural Appreciation," in The University Church of Christ the King: A Brief History. London, 1964.

87. "Architecture," in Edwardian England, 1901-1914, ed. by S. H. Nowell-Smith. London: Oxford University Press, 1964, p. 351-366.

88. "Architecture," in Studies in the History of Swindon, by L. V. Grinsell ... [and others] and John Betjeman. Swindon: Borough Council, 1950, p. 162-183.

89. "The Arrest of Oscar Wilde at the Cadogan Hotel," in Oscar Wilde: A Collection of Critical Essays, ed. by Richard Ellmann. Englewood Cliffs, N.J.: Prentice-Hall, [1969], p. 42-43.

90. "At the Back of East India Dock Road," in Gala Day London, photography by Izis Bidermanas, texts by John Betjeman [and others]. London: The Harvill Press, 1953, p. 98 and 110.
    Includes the poems:

    Through those broad streets to Whiteley's once/ and
    O had I the wings of an aeroplane/

91. "Betjeman's Britain," in The Saturday Book, ed. by John Hadfield. London: Hutchinson, 1958, v. 18, p. 78-112.

92. "Building the Museum," in Treasures of the British Museum. London: Collins, 1971, p. 14-20.

53

93. "Costa Blanca," in The Saturday Book, ed. by
    John Hadfield. London: Hutchinson, 1971; New
    York: Clarkson N. Potter, 1971, v. 31, p. 138.

94. "Evelyn Waugh," in Living Writers: Being Critical
    Studies Broadcast in the B. B. C. Third Programme,
    ed. by Gilbert Phelps. London: Sylvan Press,
    1947, p. 137-150.

95. "A Father and His Fate," in The Art of I. Compton-
    Burnett, ed. by Charles Burkhart. London: Victor
    Gollancz, 1972, p. 64-65.
    Review of A Father and His Fate by Ivy Compton-
    Burnett, reprinted from the Daily Telegraph,
    August 16, 1957.

96. "The Five Sonnets," in The Barrier, by Robin
    Maugham. London, New York: W. H. Allen,
    1973, p. 187-197.
    This is a novel containing five sonnets by John
    Betjeman written in the style of the period.
    Contains the following poems:

      I. Blow winds about the house, you cannot
         shake me, /
     II. It must be breakfast time at home today, /
    III. Adultery! The moon and stars permit it, /
     IV. Now is my heart on fire, which once was
         chilled. /
      V. Now has the utmost cruelty been done. /

97. "The Gothic Visions of Rodney Hubbock," in The
    Saturday Book, ed. by John Hadfield. London:
    Hutchinson, 1968, v. 28, p. 224-235.

98. "How to Get On in Society," in Noblesse Oblige,
    ed. by Nancy Mitford. London: H. Hamilton,
    1956; New York: Harper & Brothers, 1956,
    p. 157-159.

99. "How to Get On in Society," in Time and Tide
    Anthology. London: André Deutsch, 1956, p. 208-
    213.

This first appeared as a competition set by
John Betjeman. See also the entry in the
section "Poems in Magazines."

100. "Jacob Epstein," in Twelve Jews, ed. by Hector
Bolitho. London: Rich and Cowan, 1934, p. 83-
100.

101. _____. Freeport, New York: Books for Libraries Press, 1967, p. 83-100. (Essay Index
Series)

102. "London Railway Stations," in Flower of Cities:
A Book of London: Studies and Sketches by 22
Authors. London: M. Parrish, 1949; New
York: Harper & Brothers, 1950, p. 13-30.

103. "Lord Barton-Bendish," in The Saturday Book, ed.
by John Hadfield. London: Hutchinson, 1956,
v. 16, p. 103-104.

104. "Lord Mount Prospect," in The Second Mercury
Story Book. London, New York, Toronto: Longmans, 1931, p. 172-184.

105. _____, in The Third Omnibus of Crime, ed.
by Dorothy Sayers. New York: Coward McCann,
1935, p. 375-386.
See also entry in the section "Articles."

106. "Meditation on a Lucas Mezzotint of a Constable
Picture," in The Work of the Historic Buildings
Board by the Greater London Council, Historic
Buildings Board. London: 1970, p. 57. Cover
title: Do You Care about Historic Buildings?

107. "Middlesex," in A Map of Modern English Verse,
by John Press. London: Oxford, New York:
Oxford University Press, 1969, p. 215.

108. "Poems of the 'Nineties," chosen by John Betjeman, in The Saturday Book, ed. by John Hadfield.
London: Hutchinson, 1965, v. 25, p. 40-54.

109. "A Subaltern's Love Song," in So You're Engaged,
      ed. by Richard Muir. London: Rowse Muir Pub-
      lications, 1956, p. 14-15.

110. "Summer Poem," in The Wind and the Rain: An
      Easter Book for 1962, ed. by Neville Braybrooke.
      London: Secker & Warburg, 1962, p. 280-283.

111. "Sun and Fun: Song of a Night-Club Proprietress,"
      in The Saturday Book, ed. by John Hadfield.
      London: Macmillan, 1952, v. 12, p. 224-225.

112. "T. S. Eliot the Londoner," in T. S. Eliot: A
      Symposium for His Seventieth Birthday, ed. by
      Neville Braybrooke. New York: Farrar, Straus
      & Cudahy; London: Hart-Davis, 1958, p. 193-
      195.

113. "Tomsk-Omsk-Omsk-Tomsk" [a prose parody], in
      Parody Party, by E. C. Bentley, John Betjeman
      [and others], ed. by Leonard Russell. London:
      Hutchinson, [1936], p. 215-243.

114. "The Usher of Highgate Junior School," in T. S.
      Eliot: A Symposium. comp. by Richard March
      and Tambimuttu. London: Editions Poetry, 1948,
      p. 89-92.

115. _____, in T. S. Eliot: A Symposium, ed. by
      Richard March and Tambimuttu. Chicago: Henry
      Regnery, 1949, p. 89-92.

116. _____, in T. S. Eliot: A Symposium, ed. by
      Richard March and M. J. Tambimuttu. Chicago:
      Regnery, 1959, p. 89-92.

117. _____, in T. S. Eliot: A Symposium, ed. by
      M. J. Tambimuttu and Richard March. London:
      Frank & Cass, 1965, p. 89-92.

118. _____, in T. S. Eliot, ed. by Thurairaja Tam-
      bimuttu and Richard March. New York: Tam-
      bimuttu & Mass, 1965, p. 89-92.

E. INTRODUCTIONS AND PREFACES

119. Bertram Rota, Ltd., firm, booksellers. Poetry
from Beowulf to the End of the Nineteenth Century.
London: Bertram Rota, Ltd. at the Bookshop of
Frank Hollings, 1970. (Catalog no. 3, New series,
Summer, 1970). Introduction by Sir John Betje-
man.

120. Clark, Leonard. Prospect of Highgate and Hampstead, by Leonard Clark with photographs by John
Gay. London: The Highgate Press, 1967. Preface by John Betjeman, p. 9-11.

121. Clarke, Basil Fulford Lowther. Anglican Cathedrals outside the British Isles. London:
S. P. C. K., 1958. Foreword by John Betjeman,
p. xxi-xxii.

122. Ellis, Cuthbert Hamilton. King Steam: Selected
Railway Paintings and Drawings, by C. Hamilton
Ellis. London: Sunday Times Magazine, 1971.
Includes prefatory verse by John Betjeman ad-
dressed to the artist:
Hail! poet artist of the age of steam:/

123. Ferriday, Peter, ed. Victorian Architecture.
London: Jonathan Cape, 1963. Introduction by
John Betjeman, p. 13-16.

124. Hindley, Winifred, ed., with the assistance of
John Betjeman. A Wealth of Poetry: Selected for
the Young in Heart. London: Basil Blackwell,
1963. Introduction by John Betjeman, p. iv-v.

125. Hughes, Pennethorne. Thirty-Eight Poems by

Pennethorne Hughes, chosen and with a foreword
by Geoffrey Grigson. London: J. Baker, 1970.
Recollections of Pennethorne Hughes, by John
Betjeman, p. 10-12.

126. Mander, Ray and Mitchenson, Joe. British Music
Hall: A Story in Pictures. London: Studio
Vista, 1965. Foreword by John Betjeman, p. 6-8.

127. Mortimer, J. D., ed. An Anthology of the Home
Counties. London: Methuen, 1947. Introduction
by John Betjeman, p. vii-xi.

128. Newbolt, Sir Henry John. Selected Poems. London: Thomas Nelson & Sons, 1940. Introduction
by John Betjeman, p. ix-xv.

129. Purcell, William Ernest. Onward Christian
Soldier: A Life of Sabine Baring-Gould. London,
New York, Toronto: Longmans, 1957. Introduc-
tion by John Betjeman, p. v-vi.

130. Secker, Martin, ed. The Eighteen-Nineties: A
Period Anthology in Prose and Verse, chosen by
Martin Secker. London: The Richards Press,
1948. Introduction by John Betjeman, p. xi-xvi.

131. Squire, Sir John Collings. Collected Poems.
London: Macmillan; New York: St. Martin's
Press, 1959. Preface by John Betjeman, p. vii-ix.

132. Thomas, Ronald Stuart. Song at the Year's
Turning: Poems 1942-1954. London: Hart-Davis,
1955. Introduction by John Betjeman, p. 11-14.

133. Westminster Abbey. Radner, Pa.: The Annen-
berg School Press with the cooperation of Weiden-
feld and Nicolson, c1972. Prologue by John
Betjeman, p. 15-35.

134. Yeoman, Beryl Botterill Antonia. Anton [The car-
toons of Beryl Botterill Antonia Yeoman]. London:
New English Library, 1971. Foreword by John
Betjeman.

F. ANTHOLOGIES INCLUDING POEMS BY BETJEMAN

135. All Day Long, ed. by Pamela Whitlock. New
York: Oxford University Press, 1954.
East Anglian Bathe
Trebetherick

136. An Anthology of Commonwealth Verse, ed. by
Margaret J. O'Donnell. London: Blackie & Son,
1963.
Death in Leamington

137. An Anthology of Contemporary Verse, ed. by
Margaret J. O'Donnell. London: Blackie & Son,
1953.
In Westminster Abbey

138. An Anthology of Modern Verse, 1940-1960, ed.
by Elizabeth Jennings. London: Methuen, [1961].
Pot-Pourri from a Surrey Garden
Before the Anaesthetic

139. A Book of Comfort: An Anthology, ed. by Eliza-
beth Goudge. New York: Coward-McCann, 1964.
Christmas
Diary of a Church Mouse
In a Bath Teashop
Sunday Morning, King's Cambridge
Diary, etc. (Lines, written to order on a set
subject, to be spoken on the wireless)

140. A Brief Anthology of Poetry, ed. by Stephen F.
Fogle. New York: American Book Company,
c1951.
In Westminster Abbey

141. The Case for Poetry: A Critical Anthology, ed.

by Frederick L. Gwynn, Ralph W. Condee and
Arthur O. Lewis. 2d ed. Englewood Cliffs,
N.J.: Prentice-Hall, c1965.
In Westminster Abbey

142. A Century of Humorous Verse, 1850-1950, ed. by
Roger Lancelyn Green. New York: Dutton, 1959.
Potpourri from a Surrey Garden

143. The Chatto Book of Modern Poetry, 1915-1955,
ed. by Cecil Day-Lewis and John Lehmann. New
ed. London: Chatto & Windus, 1959.
The Old Liberals
Norfolk
Youth and Age on Beaulieu River, Hants
A Subaltern's Love Song

144. Chief Modern Poets of England and America, ed.
by Gerald D. Sanders, John H. Nelson and M. L.
Rosenthal. 4th ed. New York: Macmillan, 1962.
The Arrest of Oscar Wilde at the Cadogan Hotel
Bristol and Clifton
The Dear Old Village
Eunice
False Security
In Westminster Abbey
Incident in the Early Life of Ebenezer Jones,
    Poet, 1828, An.
Late Flowering Lust
The Licorice Fields at Pontefract
North Coast Recollections
The Town Clerk's Views
Trebetherick
Youth and Age on Beaulieu River, Hants

145. A College Book of Verse, ed. by C. F. Main.
Belmont, Calif: Wadsworth Publishing Company,
c1970.
Senex

146. Dawn and Dusk: Poems of Our Time, ed. by
Charles Causley. New York: Franklin Watts,
1963.

Harrow-on-the-Hill
Hunter Trials

147. Dylan Thomas's Choice: An Anthology of Verse
Spoken by Dylan Thomas, ed. by Ralph Maud and
Aneirin Talfan Davies. New York: New Direc-
tions, 1964, c1963.
The Arrest of Oscar Wilde at the Cadogan Hotel
A Child Ill
Pot Pourri from a Surrey Garden
Senex

148. The Earth Is the Lord's: Poems of the Spirit,
ed. by Helen Plotz. New York: Thomas Y.
Crowell, c1965.
Sunday Morning, King's Cambridge

149. Eight Lines and Under, ed. by William Cole.
New York: Macmillan, c1967.
In a Bath Teashop

150. Erotic Poetry: The Lyrics, Ballads, Idyls, and
Epics of Love--Classical to Contemporary, ed. by
William Cole. New York: Random House, 1963.
Late-flowering Lust

151. Everybody Ought to Know, ed. by Ogden Nash.
Philadelphia: J. B. Lippincott, 1961.
A Subaltern's Love Song
Trebetherick

152. Exploring Poetry, ed. by M. L. Rosenthal and
A. J. M. Smith. New York: Macmillan, c1955.
Trebetherick

153. The Faber Book of Twentieth Century Verse: An
Anthology of Verse in Britain 1900-1950, ed. by
John Heath-Stubbs and David Wright. London:
Faber and Faber, 1953.
Parliament Hill Fields
Upper Lambourne
Youth and Age on Beaulieu River, Hants

154. _____. Revised, [i. e.] 2d ed. London:
     Faber and Faber, 1965.
     Parliament Hill Fields
     Upper Lambourne
     Youth and Age on Beaulieu River, Hants

155. Fire and Sleet and Candlelight, ed. by August
     Derleth.   Sauk City, Wis.:   Arkham House, 1961.
     A Lincolnshire Tale

156. The Fireside Book of Humorous Poetry, ed. by
     William Cole.   New York: Simon and Schuster,
     1959.
     Arrogance Repressed
     Hunter Trials
     Potpourri from a Surrey Garden

157. Forms of Poetry, ed. by James L. Calderwood
     and Harold F. Toliver.   Englewood Cliffs, N. J.:
     Prentice-Hall, c1968.
     In Westminster Abbey

158. 45-60: An Anthology of English Poetry, 1945-
     1960, ed. by Thomas Blackburn.   London:
     Putnam, 1960.
     Sun and Fun
     N. W. 5 and N. 6
     A Child Ill
     Business Girls

159. Garlands for Christmas, ed. by Chad Walsh.
     New York: Macmillan, 1965.
     Christmas

160. The Golden Treasury of the Best Songs and
     Lyrical Poems in the English Language, ed. by
     Francis Turner Palgrave with additional poems
     selected by C. Day-Lewis.   London: Collins,
     1954.
     East Anglian Bathe
     Upper Lambourne

161. The Golden Treasury of the Best Songs & Lyrical

Poems in the English Language, ed. by Francis
Turner Palgrave, with a fifth book selected by
John Press. London: Oxford University Press,
1964.
The Cottage Hospital
Ireland with Emily

162. The Guinness Book of Poetry 1960-1961. London:
Putnam, 1962.
See how the wind has knocked the rambler
down/ from Summoned by Bells.

163. The Harrap Book of Modern Verse, ed. by
Maurice Wollman and Kathleen B. Parker.
London: George G. Harrap, 1959.
Parliament Hill Fields

164. The Harrap Book of Sea Verse, ed. by Ronald
Hope. London: Published in cooperation with
the Seafarers Education Service by George G.
Harrap, 1960. Also Freeport, New York: Books
for Libraries Press, 1969.
Beside the Seaside, selections

165. The Industrial Muse: The Industrial Revolution in
English Poetry, ed. by Jeremy Warburg. London:
Oxford University Press, 1958.
The Metropolitan Railway

166. Introduction to Literature: Poems, ed. by Lynn
Altenbernd and Leslie L. Lewis. New York:
Macmillan, c1963.
In Westminster Abbey

167. Invitation to Poetry: A Round of Poems from
John Skelton to Dylan Thomas, ed. by Lloyd
Frankenberg. Garden City: Doubleday, 1956.
The Arrest of Oscar Wilde at the Cadogan Hotel

168. Little Reviews Anthology, ed. by Denys Val Baker.
London: Methuen, 1949.
To My Son

169. A Little Treasury of Modern Poetry, English and
     American, ed. by Oscar Williams. New York:
     Charles Scribner's Sons, 1946.
     In Westminster Abbey

170. _____, ed. by Oscar Williams. Rev. ed.
     New York: Charles Scribner's Sons, c1950.
     In Westminster Abbey
     The Arrest of Oscar Wilde at the Cadogan Hotel

171. _____, ed. by Oscar Williams. 3rd ed. New
     York: Charles Scribner's Sons, 1970.
     The Arrest of Oscar Wilde at the Cadogan Hotel
     In Westminster Abbey

172. The Marvelous Light: Poets and Poetry, ed. by
     Helen Plotz. New York: Thomas Y. Crowell,
     c1970.
     Deal out again the dog-eared poetry books/
     from Summoned by Bells.

173. Memorable Poetry, ed. by Sir Francis Meynell.
     New York: Franklin Watts, c1965; London: The
     Nonesuch Press, c1965.
     Hunter Trials

174. Men and Women: The Poetry of Love, ed. by
     Louis Untermeyer. New York: American Heritage
     Press, c1970.
     A Subaltern's Love Song

175. The Mid-Century: English Poetry 1940-1960, ed.
     by David Wright. Middlesex: Penguin Books,
     1965.
     Upper Lambourne
     Bristol
     Youth and Age on Beaulieu River, Hants
     I. M. Walter Ramsden, ob. March 26, 1947,
          Pembroke College, Oxford

176. Modern Ballads and Story Poems, ed. by Charles
     Causley. New York: Franklin Watts, 1965;
     London: Brockhampton Press, 1964. [English

edition has the title <u>Rising Early.</u>]
A Shropshire Lad

177. <u>Modern British Poetry</u>, ed. by Louis Untermeyer.
7th rev. ed. New York: Harcourt, Brace and
Company, c1962.
The Arrest of Oscar Wilde at the Cadogan Hotel
The Cottage Hospital
Remorse
Slough

178. <u>The Modern Poets: An American-British An-</u>
<u>thology</u>, ed. by John Malcolm Brinnin and Bill
Read. New York: McGraw-Hill, 1963.
A Subaltern's Love Song
Youth and Age on Beaulieu River, Hants

179. <u>The Modern Poet's World</u>, ed. by James Reeves.
London: William Heinemann, 1957. (The Poetry
Bookshelf)
Indoor Games near Newbury

180. <u>Modern Verse in English, 1900-1950</u>, ed. by
David Cecil and Allen Tate. New York:
Macmillan, c1958.
 ·   The Cottage Hospital
St. Saviour's, Aberdeen Park, Highbury, Lon-
don, N.
Before Invasion, 1940
Sunday Afternoon Service in St. Enodoc Church,
Cornwall
Indoor Games near Newbury

181. <u>New Modern Poetry: British and American Poetry</u>
<u>since World War II</u>, ed. by Macha L. Rosenthal.
New York: Macmillan, 1967.
The Licorice Fields at Pontefract
Late-Flowering Lust

182. <u>The New Oxford Book of English Verse, 1250-</u>
<u>1950</u>, ed. by Helen Gardner. New York and
Oxford: Oxford University Press, 1972.
Death of King George V 'New King arrives in

his capital by air . . .'
Parliament Hill Fields
The Cottage Hospital

183. The New Yorker Book of Poems. New York:
The Viking Press, c1969.
Great Central Railway, Sheffield Victoria to
Banbury
In Memoriam: A. C. , R. J. O. , K. S.
In the Public Gardens
Matlock Bath

184. Nine Modern Poets: An Anthology, ed. by Edward
Loring Black. London, New York: Macmillan,
1966.
Upper Lambourne
Youth and Age on Beaulieu River, Hants
Verses Turned in Aid of St. Katherine,
Chiselhampton
Christmas
The Village Inn
Greenaway
Hertfordshire
Death in Leamington

185. The Norton Anthology of Poetry, ed. by Arthur
M. Eastman [and others]. New York: W. W.
Norton, 1970.
Blackfriars
Death in Leamington
Margate, 1940

186. The Oxford Book of Light Verse, ed. by Wystan
H. Auden. New York: Oxford University Press,
1938. Reprinted with corrections, 1939.
"New King arrives in his capital by air"
Westgate-on-Sea

187. The Oxford Book of Twentieth Century English
Verse, ed. by Philip Larkin. New York: Oxford
University Press, 1973.
The Arrest of Oscar Wilde at the Cadogan Hotel
A Subaltern's Love Song

Ireland with Emily
From Beside the Seaside
Christmas
The Metropolitan Railway
Middlesex
How to Get On in Society
Diary of a Church Mouse
Felixstowe, or, The Last of Her Order
Lord Cozens Hardy
From Summoned by Bells

188. The Penguin Book of Contemporary Verse, 1918-
1960, ed. by Kenneth Allott. New rev. ed.
Harmondsworth, Middlesex: Penguin Books, 1962.
The Planster's Vision
May-Day Song for North Oxford
Death in Leamington
The Cottage Hospital

189. The Penguin Book of Satirical Verse, ed. by
Edward Lucie-Smith. Harmondsworth, Middlesex:
Penguin Books, 1967.
Period Piece

190. Poems of the Mid-Century, ed. by John Holloway.
London: Harrap, 1957.
Seaside Golf
A Subaltern's Love Song

191. Poems of the Sixties, ed. by Frederick Edward
Simpson Finn. London: John Murray, [1970].
Inexpensive Progress
Harvest Hymn
Lines Written to Martyn Skinner before his
departure from Oxfordshire in search of
quiet--1961
By the Ninth Green, St. Enodoc
Cornish Cliffs
Agricultural Caress

192. Poems of the War Years: An Anthology, comp.
by Maurice Wollman. London: Macmillan, 1948.
Before the Anaesthetic

Bristol
Upper Lambourne

193. Poetry for Pleasure: The Hallmark Book of
     Poetry. Garden City: Doubleday, 1960.
     Death in Leamington
     The Planster's Vision
     Seaside Golf

194. Poetry in Perspective: A Critical Anthology, ed.
     by E. L. Flint and M. K. Flint. London: Uni-
     versity of London Press, 1963.
     A Subaltern's Love Song

195. Poetry of the Thirties, ed. by Robin Skelton.
     Harmondsworth, Middlesex: Penguin Books, 1964.
     Slough
     Death of King George V
     Death in Leamington
     In Westminster Abbey
     Distant View of a Provincial Town

196. Poet's Choice, ed. by Paul Engle and Joseph
     Langland. New York: The Dial Press, 1962.
     Pot-Pourri from a Surrey Garden

197. Poets of Our Time, ed. by Frederick Edward
     Simpson Finn. London: John Murray, 1965.
     Upper Lambourne
     Greenaway
     Bristol and Clifton
     In Westminster Abbey
     Sunday Morning, King's Cambridge
     The Village Inn
     Diary of a Church Mouse
     Christmas
     London from Summoned by Bells

198. Seven Centuries of Poetry, Chaucer to Dylan
     Thomas, ed. by A. N. Jeffares. London: Long-
     mans, Green, 1955.
     Before the Anaesthetic, or, A Real Fright

199. _____, ed. by A. N. Jeffares. New ed.
     London: Longmans, Green, 1960.
     Before the Anaesthetic, or, A Real Fright

200. The Sheldon Book of Verse, ed. by P. G. Smith
     and J. F. Wilkins. New York: Oxford University
     Press, 1959. Book IV.
     A Shropshire Lad
     A Subaltern's Love Song

201. The Silver Treasury of Light Verse, ed. by Oscar
     Williams. New York: New American Library,
     1957.
     The Arrest of Oscar Wilde at the Cadogan Hotel

202. Sprints and Distances: Sports in Poetry and the
     Poetry in Sports, ed. by Lillian Morrison. New
     York: Thomas Y. Crowell, c1965.
     East Anglian Bathe
     The Olympic Girl
     Seaside Golf

203. A Treasury of British Humor, ed. by Morris
     Bishop. New York: Coward-McCann, 1942.
     Distant View of a Provincial Town

204. Twentieth Century Poetry: American and British
     (1900-1970), ed. by John Malcolm Brinnin and
     Bill Read. Rev. ed. New York: McGraw-Hill,
     1970.
     A Subaltern's Love Song
     Youth and Age on Beaulieu River, Hants

205. Understanding Poetry, ed. by Cleanth Brooks and
     Robert Penn Warren. 3d ed. New York: Holt,
     1960.
     The Cottage Hospital

206. A Wealth of Poetry: Selected for the Young in
     Heart, ed. with the assistance of John Betjeman
     by Winifred Hindley. London: Basil Blackwell,
     1963.
     Business Girls

Christmas
Wantage Bells

207. What Cheer: An Anthology of American and
British Humorous and Witty Verse, ed. by David
McCord.   New York: Coward-McCann, 1945.
Also New York: Modern Library, 1955.
New King Arrives in His Capital by Air

208. Wonders and Surprises, ed. by Phyllis McGinley.
Philadelphia: Lippincott, 1968.
A Subaltern's Love Song

209. The Wordly Muse: An Anthology of Serious Light
Verse, ed. by A. J. M. Smith.   New York:
Abelard Press, c1951.
The Fête Champêtre
Potpourri from a Surrey Garden

G. POEMS IN MAGAZINES

210. "Anglo-Catholic Congresses," Christian Century, 84 (January 11, 1967), 47.

211. "Anticipation in Spring," The Listener, 27 (March 19, 1942), 358.

212. "The Archaeological Picnic," Horizon (London), 2 (September, 1940), 91.

213. "A Ballad of George R. Sims," New Statesman, n. s. 76 (October 25, 1968), 540. A review in verse of Prepare to Shed Them Now: Ballads of George R. Sims.

214. "A Bay in Anglesey," Cornhill, 174 (Winter 1964-65), 264.

215. [_____]. "John Betjeman Worksheets," The Malahat Review, 1 (1967), 130-134.

216. "Betjemania: A Poem Written for the Opening of the Exhibition of Irish Architectural Drawings at the RIBA," Royal Institute of British Architects Journal, ser. 3, 73 (February, 1966), 51.

217. "Blackfriars," Horizon (London), 1 (March, 1940), 172-173.

218. "By the Ninth Green, St. Enodoc," New Yorker, 42 (October 1, 1966), 54.

219. "Cheltenham," The Listener, 20 (December 22, 1938), 1362.

220. "A Child Ill," see "Three Poems."

221. "The Cockney Amorist," New Yorker, 34
     (April 12, 1958), 44

222. "Cornish Cliffs," New Yorker, 42 (May 21, 1966)
     46.

223. "Cornwall in Childhood," Cornhill, 171 (Fall,
     1960), 275-280.
     A preprint of a part of the author's autobio-
     graphical poem, Summoned by Bells.

224. "County," London Magazine, n. s. 8 (May, 1968),
     28-29.

225. "Crematorium," Poetry, 119 (November, 1971),
     98.

226. "Cricket Master: An Incident," London Magazine,
     7 (November, 1960), 11-13.

227. "Death in Leamington," London Mercury, 22 (May,
     1930), 14.

228. "Devonshire Street, W 1," Time and Tide, 34
     (August 8, 1953), 1039.

229. "Dorset Poem," London Mercury, 27 (December,
     1932), 110.

230. "Eunice," see "Two Poems."

231. "Executive," Encounter, 38 (January, 1972), 27.

232. "False Security," see "Two Poems."

233. "Fragment of a Poem for Emily Hemphill,"
     Cornhill, 161 (January, 1944), 19-20.

234. "Great Central Railway Sheffield Victoria to Ban-
     bury," New Yorker, 38 (March 31, 1962), 34.

235. "Greek Orthodox," London Magazine, n. s. 11
     (October/November, 1971), 54-55.

236. "Henley-on-Thames," Horizon (London), 9 (March,
     1944), 151.

237. "How to Get On in Society," Time and Tide, 32
     (December 29, 1951), 1286.
     Originally set as a competition. Competitors
     were asked to compose one more stanza. Re-
     sults appeared in Time and Tide, 33 (Jan-
     uary 19, 1952), 66. The poem was supposed
     to contain 34 of what some people might call
     social errors. For reference to many re-
     printings of these verses see the section on
     anthologies.

238. "Hundreds of birds in the air/" [poem celebrating
     the wedding of Princess Anne], Newsweek, 82
     (November 26, 1973), 50.

239. _____, Time, 102 (November 26, 1973), 50.

240. "Hunter Trials," Time and Tide, 33 (January 5,
     1952), 13.

241. "In Memoriam: A. C. , R. J. O. , K. S. " New
     Yorker, 38 (July 14, 1962), 28.

242. _____, Cornhill, 173 (Winter, 1963-64), 428-
     429.
     This poem has one more stanza than does the
     poem in the New Yorker.

243. "In the Public Gardens," New Yorker, 33 (Jan-
     uary 4, 1958), 20.

244. _____, Cornhill, 170 (Fall, 1958), 201.

245. "In Willesden Churchyard," New Yorker, 42
     (September 10, 1966), 54.

246. "Indoor Games Near Newbury," New Statesman

74 Sir John Betjeman

and Nation, n. s. 33 (January 18, 1947), 48.

247. "The Irish Unionist's Farewell to Greta Hellström
in 1922," Cornhill, 161 (December, 1945), 479-
480.

248. "The Licorice Fields at Pontefract," New Statesman and Nation, 39 (March 18, 1950), 306.

249. "A Lincolnshire Tale," Cornhill, 161 (April,
1945), 312-313.

250. "Lines Written to Martyn Skinner," Harper's
Magazine, 229 (September, 1964), 72.

251. "A Literary Discovery," Time and Tide, 33
(December 6, 1952), 1434, 1436.

252. "Loneliness," New Yorker, 47 (April 17, 1971),
45.

253. "Margate," The Listener, 24 (October 24, 1940),
587.

254. "Matlock Bath," New Yorker, 35 (March 14,
(1959), 40.

255. _____, Cornhill, 170 (Summer, 1959), 414-415.

256. "May Day Song for North Oxford," Horizon (London), 12 (July, 1945), 10-11.

257. "Mortality," Encounter, 25 (July, 1965), 28.

258. "N.W. 5 & N. 6," Cornhill, 169 (Winter, 1957-58),
429-430.

259. "Narcissus," London Magazine, n. s. 5 (June,
1965), 56-57.

260. "Not Necessarily Leeds," Spectator, 193
(October 1, 1954), 392.

261. "The Old Liberals," Horizon (London), 19 (April, 1949), 231.

262. "Olympic Girl," Harper's Magazine, 212 (January, 1956), 55.

263. "On a Late Victorian Water Colour of Oxford," Horizon (London), 7 (April, 1943), 223.

264. "On a Painting by Julius Olsson, R. A." London Magazine, n. s. 11 (August/September, 1971), 94-95.

265. "On Leaving Wantage July 1972," London Magazine, n. s. 12 (October/November, 1972), 5.

266. "One and All," Daily Telegraph, June 2, 1967, p. 32.

267. "Original Sin on the Sussex Coast: A Jolly Christmas Message," Time and Tide, 32 (December 8, 1951), 1195.

268. "The P. R. O. ," London Magazine, n. s. 10 (July/August, 1970), 106-110.

269. "Parliament Hill Fields," New Statesman & Nation, 19 (February 24, 1940), 240.

270. "Period Piece," London Magazine, n. s. 4 (June, 1964), 19-20.

271. "A Plain Course on the Bells," Horizon (London), 11 (February, 1945), 81.

272. "Poems in the Porch," The Listener, 53 (February 10, 1955), 253.
    "Now is the time when we recall/ The sharp conversion of St. Paul/, "... a contribution in rhyme to the controversy aroused by Mrs. Knight's broadcasts."

273. "The Poplars are fell'd, farewell to the shade,"

The Times (London), August 13, 1970, p. 6f.

274. "Pot Pourri from a Surrey Garden," New States-
     man & Nation, 16 (November 12, 1938), 777.

275. "Remorse," Time and Tide, 34 (October 17,
     1953), 1346.

276. "St. Saviour's Aberdeen Park, Highbury, London,
     N.," Architectural Review, 104 (December, 1948),
     307.

277. "Sand in the Sandwiches, Wasps in the Tea," ex-
     cerpts from four poems, Newsweek, 80
     (October 23, 1972), 60.

278. "Seaside Golf," see "Three Poems."

279. "Small Town of Ireland: A 'Hedge Poem,'"
     Weekend Telegraph, January 21, 1966, p. 24-26.

280. "A Subaltern's Love Song," Horizon (London), 3
     (February, 1941), 148-149.

281. _____, New York Times Magazine, August 13,
     1967, p. 25.

282. _____, Sunday Times Colour Supplement (Lon-
     don), August 8, 1965, p. 16.

283. "Summoned by Bells," New Yorker, 36 (August 27,
     1960), 31-42.

284. "Sunday Afternoon Service," Cornhill, 161 (Novem-
     ber, 1944), 210-212.

285. "Sunday Morning, King's Cambridge," Atlantic
     Monthly, 194 (September, 1954), 65.

286. "Three Poems: The Weary Journalist; Seaside
     Golf; A Child Ill," Harper's Magazine, 213
     (July, 1956), 69.

287. "Tregardock," Atlantic, 217 (February, 1966), 89.

288. "Two Poems: False Security; and Eunice," London Magazine, 2 (May, 1955), 30-31.

289. "Upper Lambourne," Horizon (London), 1 (January, 1940), 12.

290. "Variation on a Theme by Newbolt," London Magazine, 3 (May, 1956), 15.

291. "Village Wedding," New Yorker, 35 (July 11, 1959), 30.

292. _____, Cornhill, 171 (Winter, 1959-60), 92.

293. "The Weary Journalist," Time and Tide, 31 (December 2, 1950), 1198.

294. _____, see also "Three Poems."

295. "A Wembley Lad," New Statesman, 82 (November 12, 1971), 658.

296. "Winter Seascape," Ladies Home Journal, 88 (February, 1971), 126.

297. "Wykehamist at Home," Review of Reviews (London), 85 (July, 1934), 89.

298. "Ye Olde Cottage," The Heretick No. 2, Marlborough College, 1924.

299. "Youth and Age on Beaulieu River, Hants," New Statesman and Nation, 30 (October 6, 1945), 228.

H. ARTICLES

300. "Aberdeen Granite," The Listener, 38 (August 7, 1947), 213-218.

301. "Architecture," London Mercury, 29 (November, 1933), 65-67.

302. "As Far as Stone Would Go," Daily Telegraph, November 20, 1970, Colour Supplement, p. 58+.

303. "Australia: Everything Is Different," Vogue, 142 (December, 1963), 182-183.

304. "Author of 'Onward, Christian Soldiers,' " The Listener, 34 (November 8, 1945), 517.

305. "Back to the Railway Carriage," The Listener, 23 (March 28, 1940), 621-622.

306. "Baillie Scott and the 'Architecture of Escape,' " Studio (London), 116 (October, 1938), 177-180.

307. "Bastions of Power and Refuges of Learning," Daily Telegraph, October 30, 1970, Colour Supplement, p. 30.

308. "Before the Normans Came," Daily Telegraph, October 23, 1970, Colour Supplement, p. 40-46.

309. "Betjeman and Milligan on Melancholia," Sunday Times Magazine, August 8, 1965, p. 16-21.

310. "Betjeman on Padstow," Architectural Review, 112 (December, 1952), 411.

311. "Between Us and the Human Anthill," Daily Telegraph, June 25, 1971, Colour Supplement, p. 26.

312. "Billy Graham," Spectator, 192 (March 12, 1954), 282.

313. "Birmingham's Who's Who," Time and Tide, 34 (July 11, 1953), 919-920.

314. "Blurbs," Time and Tide, 31 (October 31, 1950), 1052.

315. "Bristol: An Unspoiled City," The Listener, 17 (April 28, 1937), 825.

316. "C. F. A. Voysey," Architectural Forum, 72 (May, 1940), 348-349.

317. "A Century of English Architecture," Spectator, 209 (August 24, 1962), 252-254.

318. "Charles Francis Annesley Voysey," Architectural Review, 70 (October, 1931), 93-96.

319. "Church-Crawling," The Listener, 40 (August 12, 1948), 227-228.

320. "Church Restoration," Spectator, 159 (October 22, 1937), 683.

321. "City and Suburban," see weekly issues of Spectator, 193 (October 15, 1954) through 200 (January 10, 1958).
    Essays on miscellaneous topics. By January 1958 the weekly essay had become a burden to the author. A lament in verse by H. J. Hammerton in the form of a letter to the editor appears in Spectator, 200 (January 17, 1958), 73.

322. "City and Suburban," Spectator, 203 (November 20, 1959), 697.

323. "The City Churches," Spectator, 193 (November 5, 1954), xxxi-xxxii.

324. "A Connoisseur of Old Books," The Listener, 61 (March 5, 1959), 405-406.

325. "Conservatories and Other Edwardiana," The Listener, 73 (February 4, 1965), 194-195. Written in collaboration with Osbert Lancaster.

326. "Cooke of Cookesborough," The Listener, 18 (October 13, 1937), 791-792.

326a. "The Criterion Theatre (Opened 1874)," Connoisseur, 185 (January, 1974), 17-21.

327. "Dead from the Waist Down," Spectator, 200 (March 14, 1958), 320-321.

328. "The Death of Modernism," Architectural Review, 70 (December, 1931), 161.

329. "Dictating to the Railways," Architectural Review, 74 (September, 1933), 83-84.

330. "1830-1930--Still Going Strong," Architectural Review, 67 (May, 1930), 230-240.

331. "1837-1937: A Spiritual Change Is the One Hope for Art," Studio (London), 113 (February, 1937), 56-73.

332. "Face to Face with Myself: Today ... John Betjeman," Daily Herald, March 8, 1961, p. 4.

333. "The Festival Buildings," Time and Tide, 32 (May 5, 1951), 392-393.

334. " 'For ever England,' " The Listener, 75 (February 3, 1966), 165-167. In collaboration with Osbert Lancaster.

335. "Fulham Grange," Spectator, 193 (July 16, 1954), 75.

336. "Game of Snakes and Ladders to Literary Success," Time and Tide, 31 (December 2, 1950), 1218, 1221. In collaboration with Osbert Lancaster.

337. "Georgian Exeter," The Listener, 17 (June 23, 1937), 1243.

338. "Glories of English Craftsmanship--Electricity and Old Churches," Time and Tide, 34 (December 5, 1953), 1582-1583.

339. "The Gorell Report," Architectural Review, 72 (July, 1932), 13-14.

340. "Gothic: A Moral Superiority," Daily Telegraph, June 11, 1971, Supplement, p. 30.

341. "Guano and Golden Eagles," Spectator, 200 (May 16, 1958), 616-617.

342. "A Holy Exuberance," Daily Telegraph, November 13, 1970, Colour Supplement, p. 60+.

343. "Honour Your Forbears," Read before the R.I.B.A. on January 5, 1954, Royal Institute of British Architects Journal, ser. 3, 61 (January, 1954), 87-91. Discussion, p. 91-93.

344. "How to Look at a Church," The Listener, 20 (September 8, 1938), 484-486.

345. "How to Look at Books," The Listener, 22 (August 31, 1939), 442.

346. "An Irreplaceable House," The Listener, 66 (October 19, 1961), 593.

347. "John Betjeman Replies," Spectator, 193 (October 8, 1954), 441.

348. "John Bull's First Job: Failed in Divinity," Spectator, 211 (November 29, 1963), 687.

349. "The Kingdom of the Mind," The Listener, 24
     (December 12, 1940), 837.

350. "Leeds, a City of Contrasts," Architectural
     Review, 74 (October, 1933), 129-138.

351. "Letcombe Bassett," Architectural Review, 105
     (June, 1949), 307-308.

352. "Literary History and Criticism," London Mer-
     cury, 28 (May, 1933), 85-87.

353. "Lord Berners, 1883-1950," The Listener, 43
     (May 11, 1950), 839.

354. "Lord Mount Prospect" [a story], London Mercury,
     21 (December, 1929), 113-121.

355. "Louis MacNeice and Bernard Spencer," London
     Magazine, n. s. 3 (December, 1963), 62-64.

356. "Lunch at the Stores," London Mercury, 28
     (August, 1933), 344-347.

357. "M. H. Baillie Scott, F. R. I. B. A., an Apprecia-
     tion," Studio (London), 130 (July, 1945), 17.

358. "Mackay Hugh Baillie Scott," Manx Museum
     Journal, 7 (1968), 77-80.

359. "The Magic of Cornwall," Holiday, 29 (June,
     1961), 58-63, 135-136.

360. "A Martyr to Income Tax," Time and Tide, 32
     (June 16, 1951), 563.

361. "Memorial to a Great Architect [Sir Edwin
     Lutyens], Country Life, 109 (February 2, 1951),
     324-325.

362. "Necessity: Mother of the Pointed Arch," Daily
     Telegraph, November 6, 1970, Colour Supple-
     ment, p. 34+.

363. "The New Chair of Art," Architectural Review,
       68 (December, 1930), 235.

364. "A New Westminster," Spectator, 201 (Novem-
       ber 21, 1958), 684.

365. "Nonconformist Architecture," Architectural
       Review, 88 (December, 1940), 161-174.

366. "Note on J. N. Comper," Architectural Review,
       85 (February, 1939), 79-82.

367. "Note on James Wyatt," Architectural Review,
       71 (March, 1932), 97-98.

368. " 'Oh, to be in England ...' " The Listener, 29
       (March 11, 1943), 295-296.

369. "P. Morton Shand," Architectural Review, 128
       (November, 1960), 325-328.

370. "Parson Hawker, Cornish Mystic," The Listener,
       34 (October 18, 1945), 438-439.

371. "The Passing of the Village," Architectural
       Review, 72 (September, 1932), 89-93.

372. "Pavillioned in Splendour," Daily Telegraph,
       June 4, 1971, Colour Supplement, p. 30+.

373. "Penalties of Success," The Author, 78 (Spring,
       1967), 9-10.

374. "The Persecution of Country Clergy," Time and
       Tide, 32 (March 17, 1951), 231.

375. "Piers of the Realm," Daily Telegraph,
       August 6, 1971, Magazine, p. 33-34.

376. "Piranesian Visions of Today," Country Life,
       143 (May 9, 1968), 1226-1229.

377. "The Pleasures of Book-Hunting," The Listener,

84   Sir John Betjeman

30 (December 2, 1943), 641-642.

378. "Private Comfort and Public Pomp," Daily
Telegraph, June 18, 1971, Colour Supplement,
p. 30.

379. "Progress in Advertising," Gebrauchsgraphik, 14
(March, 1937), 36-37.
In German and English. Translated into Ger-
man by L. Fritz Gruber.

380. "Prosperity in Stone. Confidence in Mortar,"
Daily Telegraph, November 27, 1970, Colour
Supplement, p. 58+.

381. "The Rhyme and Reason of Verse," Daily Telegraph Magazine, January 8, 1971, p. 30.

382. "The Seeing Eye: or, How to Like Everything,"
Architectural Review, 86 (November, 1939), 201-
204.

383. "Seeking Whom He May Devour," The Listener,
37 (January 9, 1947), 75.

384. "Selling Our Churches," Spectator, 192 (April 2,
1954), 383-384.

385. "A Sense of Proportions," Daily Telegraph,
May 28, 1971, Colour Supplement, p. 34+.

386. "Sermons That Ruined the Carrot Crop," The
Listener, 21 (February 23, 1939), 407-408.

387. "Sezincote, Moreton-in-Marsh, Gloucestershire:
Its Situation, History and Architecture," Architectural Review, 69 (May, 1931), 161-166e.

388. "Sir Henry Newbolt after a Hundred Years," The
Listener, 67 (June 28, 1962), 1114-1115.

389. "A Spectator's Notebook," Spectator, 193
(August 27, 1954), 244, and (September 3, 1954),
272.

390. "Street Furniture," Journal of the Royal Society of Arts, 105 (December, 1956), 110-116.

391. "Swindon: British Towns and Cities, XII," History Today, 2 (May, 1952), 351-357.

392. "There and Back: 1851 A.D. to 1933 A.D.: A History of the Revival of Good Craftsmanship," Architectural Review, 74 (July, 1933), 4-8.

393. "A Tribute to Wystan Auden," in "Five," by Robert Lowell and others, Shenandoah, 18 (Winter, 1967), 45-57.

394. "The Truth about Waterloo Bridge," Architectural Review, 71 (April, 1932), 125-127.

395. "Two Cornish Houses," Architectural Review, 73 (April, 1933), 153-158.

396. "Using One's Eyes," The Listener, 67 (January 18, 1962), 117-118.

397. "Victorian Architecture," World Review, n. s. 23 (January, 1951), 46-52.

398. "Vintage London," New Statesman and Nation, n. s. 24 (December 26, 1942), 425-426.

399. "Wolf's Cove, Thirlwall Mere, & District," Architectural Review, 71 (January, 1932), 8-11.

400. "Working to Rules," Daily Telegraph, May 21, 1971, Colour Supplement, p. 39+.

I. REVIEWS BY JOHN BETJEMAN

401. "Amy in Brodieland," Spectator, 222 (April 18, 1969), 508.
A review of Seventh Child, by Amy Barlow.

402. "And Did Those Feet ...," Spectator, 221 (October 25, 1968), 583.
A review of Wyndham and Children First, by Lord Egremont.

403. "Antiquarian Prejudice," New Statesman and Nation, n.s. 14 (October 23, 1937), 656.
A review of Middlesex, by the Royal Commission on Historical Manuscripts.

404. "Architecture in Fiction," Architectural Review, 76 (November, 1934), 174-175.
A review of A Handful of Dust, by Evelyn Waugh.

405. "The Beauty of Bristol," Time and Tide, 33 (March 15, 1952), 254-255.
A review of The Georgian Buildings of Bristol, by Walter Ison.

406. "Belles-Lettres--I," London Mercury, 30 (June, 1934), 171-173.
A review of six books of description of the English countryside.

407. "Books: American Folk Art," New Yorker, 33 (December 28, 1957), 66+.
A review of The Gingerbread Age, by John Maass.

408. "Books: Banker's Georgian and Coca-Colonial,"
     New Yorker, 34 (December 13, 1958), 211-212,
     214.
        A review of Here, of all Places, by Osbert
     Lancaster.

409. "Books from My Stocking," Spectator, 199
     (November 22, 1957), 710-711.
        A review of six books on house decoration and
     related subjects.

410. "Books: Pilgrim's Progress," New Yorker, 36
     (April 23, 1960), 174-177.
        A review of Monsignor Ronald Knox, by
     Evelyn Waugh.

411. "Common Experiences," The Listener, 71
     (March 19, 1964), 483.
        A review of The Whitsun Weddings by Philip
     Larkin.

412. "Dead Knights and Ladies," Spectator, 165
     (December 13, 1940), 652.
        A review of Alabaster Tombs of the Pre-
     Reformation Period in England, by Arthur
     Gardner.

413. "The Diary of a Somebody," Time and Tide, 31
     (August 26, 1950), 856-857.
        A review of Recollections, by Thomas Graham
     Jackson.

414. "Early Victorian Architecture," Spectator, 194
     (May 6, 1955), 591-592.
        A review of Early Victorian Architecture in
     Britain, by Henry-Russell Hitchcock.

415. "Enclosures Green," Spectator, 216 (June 10,
     1966), 732.
        A review of English Landscaping and Literature,
     1660-1840, by Edward Malins and Studies in
     Landscape Design, Vol. II, by G. A. Jellico.

416. "End of the Line," Spectator, 215 (July 9, 1965),
     53-54.
        A review of British Branch Lines, by H. A.
     Vallance and The Future of Britain's Railways,
     by Roger Calvert.

417. "English Baroque," New Statesman and Nation,
     n. s. 21 (January 25, 1941), 92.
        A review of Country House Baroque, by
     Anthony Ayscough [and others].

418. "English Church Screens," New Statesman and
     Nation, n. s. 12 (October 3, 1936), 480.
        A review of English Church Screens, by
     Aylmer Vallance.

419. "English Decoration," Time and Tide, 33
     (May 10, 1952), 488.
        A review of Decoration and Furniture, Vol. I:
     The English Tradition, by Bruce Allsopp.

420. "Every London Church," Spectator, 217 (Octo-
     ber 28, 1966), 554-555.
        A review of Parish Churches of London, by
     Basil F. L. Clarke.

421. "Eye for a Church," Time and Tide, 33 (Novem-
     ber 1, 1952), 1274.
        A review of English Parish Churches, by
     Graham Hutton.

422. "F. J. Harvey Darton," New Statesman and
     Nation, n. s. 12 (August 1, 1936), 166, 168.
        A review of Alibi Pilgrimage, by F. J. Harvey
     Darton.

423. "Fanfarlo," New Statesman and Nation, n. s. 26
     (November 27, 1943), 357.
        A review of Shaving Through the Blitz, by
     G. W. Stonier.

424. "Faraway Fairways," Time and Tide, 33
     (April 26, 1952), 420-421.

A review of <u>A History of Golf in Britain</u>, by Bernard Darwin.

425. "Flashing Facets," <u>New Statesman and Nation</u>, n. s. 17 (March 11, 1939), 390-392.
A review of <u>Let Dons Delight</u>, by Ronald Knox.

426. "Funny Books," <u>New Statesman and Nation</u>, n. s. 16 (December 3, 1938), 932, 934.
A review of six humorous books.

427. _____, <u>New Statesman and Nation</u>, n. s. 18 (December 9, 1939), 840, 842.
A review of ten humorous books.

428. "Gardener in Glass," <u>Spectator</u>, 208 (January 19, 1962), 77-78.
A review of <u>The Works of Sir Joseph Paxton, 1803-1865</u>, by George F. Chadwick.

429. "A Good Antiquarian," <u>Spectator</u>, 165 (November 22, 1940), 546, 548.
A review of <u>Design for a Journey</u>, by M. D. Anderson.

430. "A Good Boy's Story," <u>New Statesman and Nation</u>, n. s. 20 (December 7, 1940), 578, 580.
A review of seven books for boys.

431. "Gothic Patterns," <u>New Statesman</u>, 78 (August 15, 1969), 216-217.
A review of three volumes on architecture by A. W. N. Pugin.

432. "The Graver Side of School Life," <u>Architectural Review</u>, 66 (December, 1929), 297-299.
A review of <u>The English Tradition of Education</u>, by Cyril Norwood.

433. "Guide Books," <u>Time and Tide</u>, 32 (June 23, 1951), 600-601.
A review of 11 guide books.

434. "Joke-English," New Statesman and Nation, n. s.
     16 (October 22, 1938), 628.
     A review of The Speaker's Desk Book, by
     Martha Lupton.

435. "A Little Old Fashioned?" New Statesman and
     Nation, n. s. 32 (October 19, 1946), 286.
     A review of Industrial Arts Explained, by
     John Gloag.

436. "London Pleasure," Spectator, 198 (May 24,
     1957), 683-684.
     A review of The Buildings of England: London.
     Vol. I, The Cities of London and Westminster,
     by Nikolaus Pevsner.

437. "Lucky Wellingtonians," Architectural Review, 96
     (October, 1944), 155-156.
     A review of A Victorian School, by R. St.
     C. Talboys.

438. "Mither Tongue," Time and Tide, 33 (July 5,
     1952), 748.
     A review of Scottish Verse, 1851-1951, selected
     by Douglas Young.

439. "Neckwear," London Magazine, n. s. 9 (April,
     1959), 105-107.
     A review of School, University, Navy, Army,
     Air-Force & Club Ties.

440. "New College Glass," Time and Tide, 32 (July 7,
     1951), 647.
     A review article evoked by publication of The
     Stained Glass of New College, by Christopher
     Woodforde.

441. "No Longer the Vogue," Spectator, 200
     (January 24, 1958), 109-110.
     A review of Guide to Western Architecture,
     by John Gloag.

442. "Not Lewis Carroll," Time and Tide, 34 (Decem-
     ber 12, 1953), 1650.

A review of Teapots and Quails, by Edward Lear.

443. _____, in Time and Tide Anthology. London:
André Deutsch, 1956, p. 267-269.

444. "Only an Idea," Time and Tide, 32 (October 13,
1951), 975.
A review of Literary Britain, photographed by
Bill Brandt.

445. "Onwards from Dr. Watts," New Statesman and
Nation, n. s. 18 (September 16, 1939), 406-407.
A review of Cautionary Verses, by Hilaire
Belloc.

446. "The Open Air," New Statesman and Nation, n. s.
12 (July 18, 1936), 94, 96.
A review of The Open Air, an Anthology of
English Country Life, by Adrian Bell.

447. "The Pleasance That Was London," Spectator,
224 (March 21, 1970), 385-386.
A review of The Survey of London, Vol. XXXV
and London Street Views, 1838-1940, edited by
Peter Jackson.

448. "Prolific Scott," New Statesman, 80 (August 21,
1970), 212-213.
A review of Mr. Loudon's England, by John
Gloag.

449. "Quill or Mashie?" New Statesman and Nation,
n. s. 16 (July 30, 1938), 193-194.
A review of The ABC of Authorship, by Ursula
Bloom, and Family Golf, by Eleanor E. Helme.

450. "Romantic Sights," New Statesman, 76 (August 30,
1968), 260-261.
A review of Wonders of Britain, by Eric
Newby and Diana Petry.

451. "Round England," New Statesman and Nation, n. s.
12 (July 11, 1936), 58.
A review of six British travel books.

452. "Round the Bend," Spectator, 199 (August 9, 1957), 197-198.
     A review of Branch Lines, by O. S. Nock.

453. "Sermons from Heart and Head," Spectator, 214 (March 26, 1965), 402.
     A review of The True Wilderness, by H. A. Williams.

454. "Shorter Notices," Time and Tide, 33 (May 17, 1952), 528.
     A review of Community Farm, by John Middleton Murry; Portrait of an Admiral, by A. J. Marder; and Cheltenham, by Bryan Little.

455. "The Splendour Falls ...," New Statesman and Nation, n. s. 11 (June 20, 1936), 997.
     A review of The English Castle, by Hugh Braun.

456. "Steam, Speed and the Artist," New Statesman, 76 (July 5, 1968), 15.
     A review of Art and the Industrial Revolution, by Francis Klingender and Historians of London, by Stanley Rubinstein.

457. "Storied Urns and Animated Busts," Time and Tide, 34 (October 17, 1953), 1358-1359.
     A review of A Dictionary of British Sculptors, 1660-1851, by Rupert Gunnis.

458. "The Ten Storey Town," New Statesman and Nation, n. s. 10 (August 24, 1935), 254-255.
     A review of The New Architecture and the Bauhaus, by Walter Gropius.

459. "The Thames," Time and Tide, 33 (January 12, 1952), 40.
     A review of The Thames from Mouth to Source, by L. T. C. Rolt.

460. "Torture and Death," New Statesman and Nation, n. s. 16 (December 10, 1938), 982, 984.

A review of twenty-two books for boys.

461. "Trivia Anglicana," Time and Tide, 34 (May 2, 1953), 584, 586.
    A review of four pamphlets: The Church in Construction; Parish Fashions; What the Vicar Likes; and Douglas at Play.

462. "Urbanities," New Statesman, 81 (January 8, 1971), 52-53.
    A review of Nottingham, by Geoffrey Trease; Holborn, by John Lehmann; and Reading, by Alan Wykes.

463. "Victorian Book Design and Colour Printing," Spectator, 210 (May 3, 1963), 579.
    A review of Victorian Book Design and Colour Printing, by Ruari McLean.

464. "With a Lady for a Wife," London Magazine, n.s. 9 (January, 1970), 116-119.
    A review of Forty Years On: An Anthology of School Songs, compiled by Gavin Ewart.

465. "Writ in Water," Time and Tide, 33 (July 19, 1952), 818-819.
    A review of Romantic Landscape, by Paul Dehn.

No attempt has been made to list the many reviews which appeared in the Daily Telegraph between 1951 and 1967.

J. RECORDINGS

466. The Poems of John Betjeman: The Golden
Treasury of John Betjeman. Spoken Arts 710,
819. Volumes 1 and 2. 33-1/3. Read by the
author.
Contains these poems:

Volume I Spoken Arts 710
False Security
Hunter Trials
Seaside Golf
North Coast Recollections
Norfolk
Sunday in Ireland
Remorse
Youth and Age on Beaulieu River
A Subaltern's Love Song
Reproof Deserved, or, After the Lecture
Beside the Seaside
Business Women
House of Rest
Sun and Fun: Song of a Night-Club
    Proprietress
The Licorice Fields at Pontefract

Volume II Spoken Arts 819
A Lincolnshire Church
The Arrest of Oscar Wilde
The Attempt
Devonshire St., W.1
Eunice
The Last of Her Order
Harrow-on-the-Hill
The Heart of Thomas Hardy
I. M. Walter Ramsden

In a Bath Teashop
The Irish Unionist's Farewell
Matlock Bath
Middlesex
Pot Pourri from a Surrey Garden
Trebetherick
Upper Lambourne
Wantage Bells

467. Poems. Argo PLP 1067. 33-1/3. Read by the poet.
Contains these poems:

Middlesex
Harrow-on-the-Hill
Upper Lambourne
Wantage Bells
Trebetherick
The Heart of Thomas Hardy
The Arrest of Oscar Wilde
I. M. Walter Ramsden
Devonshire Street, W.1
In a Bath Teashop
The Attempt
The Irish Unionist's Farewell
A Lincolnshire Church
Pot Pourri from a Surrey Garden
Henley-on-Thames
Diary of a Church Mouse
In the Public Gardens
Eunice
The Last of Her Order
Matlock Bath

468. Summoned by Bells. Argo PLP 1069. 33-1/3.
Selections from the autobiographical poem read by the poet.

Betjeman Works Included with the Works of Others

469. Britain's Cathedrals and Their Music. London:

BBC Radio Enterprises. Volumes 1-3. BBC
1005 M REB 33 M, 61M. 33-1/3.
Contents: No. 1. Chichester and Guildford.
No. 2. Peterborough and Liverpool. No. 3.
St. Albans and Ely. Choral works and organ
music performed by the various choirs and
organists of the cathedrals with narration by
John Betjeman.

470. Donat, Robert. Robert Donat Reads His Favourite
Poems at Home. Spoken Arts RG 192. 33-1/3.
Christmas, by John Betjeman

471. Futterer, Agnes E. Exquisite Yellow: Agnes
Futterer reading a collection of Light Verse.
Theatre Alumni Association of the University of
the State of New York at Albany. MG 201, 516-
517. 33-1/3.
Westminster Abbey, by John Betjeman.

472. Guinness, Alec. Christian Poetry and Prose,
selected and read by Alec Guinness. Folkways
FL 9893 A and B. 33-1/3.
Christmas, by John Betjeman

473. The Jupiter Anthology of 20th Century English
Poetry, directed by V. C. Clinton-Baddeley.
Jupiter Recordings Ltd. Volume II. JUR 00A2.
Folkways FL 9887. John Betjeman reads his own
poems.
The Church's Restoration
The Olympic Girl

474. Lennon, Florence Becker. Enjoyment of Poetry,
broadcast over Radio Station WEVD, New York
City, June 7, 1959. Library of Congress LWO
3993, reel 3, side B. A tape recording.
Wantage Bells, by John Betjeman.

475. The Poet Speaks, Volume 7. Argo PLP 1087.
33-1/3. The poets read and discuss their own
works. Recorded in association with the British
Council and the Poetry Room in the Lamont

Library of Harvard University.
Contains the poems:

A Shropshire Lad
Before the Anaesthetic
Late Flowering Lust
The Metropolitan Railway

476. Thomas, Dylan. An Evening with Dylan Thomas,
reading his own and other poems.   Caedmon
TC 1157.   33-1/3.
To My Son, Aged Eight, by John Betjeman.

PART II

WRITINGS ABOUT
JOHN BETJEMAN

A. BIOGRAPHY AND CRITICISM: BOOKS

477. Allsop, Kenneth. Scan. London: Hodder and Stoughton, 1965, p. 24-28.

478. Auden, Wystan H. Introduction to Slick But Not Streamlined, by John Betjeman. Garden City: Doubleday, 1947, p. 9-16.

479. Beaton, Cecil Walter Hardy and Tynan, Kenneth. Persona Grata. New York: Putnam, 1954, p. 12-15.

480. Birkenhead, Frederick Winston Furneaux Smith, 2d Earl of. Introduction to John Betjeman's Collected Poems. London: John Murray, 1958, p. xiii-xxvi; also Enl. [3rd ed.]. London: Murray, 1970, p. xv-xxx.

481. Black, Edward Loring, ed. Nine Modern Poets: An Anthology. London, New York: Macmillan, 1966, p. 67-71, 205-207.

482. Blackburn, Thomas. The Price of an Eye. London: Longmans, Green & Company, 1961, p. 112-113.

483. Bogan, Louise, "John Betjeman," in Selected Criticism; Prose, Poetry, by Louise Bogan. New York: Noonday Press, 1955, p. 343-345.

484. Bowra, C. M. Memories, 1898-1939. Cambridge: Harvard University Press, 1967, p. 165-172.

485. Brooke, Jocelyn. Ronald Firbank and John

Betjeman. [London]: Published for the British
Council and the National Book League by Long-
mans, Green & Co., 1962. (Bibliographical
Series of Supplements to British Book News on
Writers and Their Work, No. 153).
Reviewed by Philip Larkin in Spectator, 210
(February 15, 1963), 200.

486. Bunnell, William S., ed. Ten Twentieth Century
Poets. Notes on Chosen English Texts by Nor-
man T. Carrington. Bath [England]: J. Brodie,
1963, p. 15-20.

487. Connolly, Cyril, ed. The Modern Movement:
One Hundred Key Books from England, France
and America, 1880-1950, chosen by Cyril
Connolly. London: Deutsch, Hamish Hamilton,
1965.
The book chosen is John Betjeman's Selected
Poems.

488. Contemporary Authors. Detroit: The Gale Research Company, 1965-1972. 32 vols. in 18.
Vol. 11-12, 1965, p. 39.

488a. Contemporary Literary Criticism. Detroit: Gale
Research, 1973. Vol. 2, p. 60-61.

489. Contemporary Poets of the English Language, ed.
by Rosalie Murphy. Chicago and London: St.
James Press, 1970, p. 89-91.
Includes an essay by William Plomer, p. 89-91.

490. Current Biography, 34 (March, 1973), 3-5. New
York: H. W. Wilson, 1973.

491. Finn, Frederick Edward Simpson. Poets of Our
Time. London: John Murray, 1965, p. 1-2.

492. Fraser, George Sutherland. The Modern Writer
and His World. London: Verschoyle, 1953; New
York, Washington: Frederick A. Praeger, 1965,
p. 306-312.

493. Henderson, Philip, "The Best of Betjeman,"
     Feature Articles Service, Radio Script 121,
     unpublished, for British Council, July 1961.

494. Jennings, Elizabeth. Poetry Today (1957-1960).
     London: Published for the British Book Council,
     by Longmans, 1961, p. 28-30, 59.   Portrait be-
     tween p. 36 and 37.   (Bibliographical Series of
     Supplements to British Book News)

495. Kermode, Frank, "Henry Miller and John Betje-
     man," in Puzzles and Epiphanies: Essays and
     Reviews, 1958-1961, by Frank Kermode.   New
     York: Chilmark Press, 1962, p. 140-154.   Also
     London: Routledge & Kegan Paul, 1962.

496. Kunitz, Stanley J., ed. Twentieth Century
     Authors: 1st Supplement. New York: H. W.
     Wilson, 1955, p. 86.

497. Larkin, Philip. Introduction to John Betjeman's
     Collected Poems, enl. ed. Boston: Houghton
     Mifflin, 1971, p. xvii-xli.

498. Nicolson, Harold. Diaries and Letters, Volume
     II, 1945-1962. London: Collins, New York:
     Atheneum, 1968, p. 243.

499. The Penguin Companion to English Literature, ed.
     by David Daiches. New York: McGraw-Hill,
     1971, p. 48.

500. Press, John. A Map of Modern English Verse.
     London; Oxford, New York: Oxford University
     Press, 1969, p. 203-204, 215.

501. _____. Rule and Energy: Trends in British
     Poetry since the Second World War. London:
     Oxford University Press, 1963, p. 7-9, 97-98,
     147.

502. The Reader's Adviser: A Guide to the Best in
     Literature, ed. by Winifred F. Courtney.   11th

ed. rev. and enl. New York: R. R. Bowker, 1968, vol. I, p. 165.

503. Rosenthal, Macha Louis. The Modern Poets: A Critical Introduction. London, Oxford, New York: Oxford University Press, 1960, p. 220-222, 224-225.

504. Ross, Alan. Poetry: 1945-1950. London: Published for the British Council by Longmans, Green, 1951, p. 50-53.

505. Schröder, Reinhard. Die Lyrik John Betjemans. Hamburg: Helmut Buske Verlag, 1972. (Hamburger Philologische Studien no. 26) Dissertation, Hamburg, 1972.

506. Sieveking, Lance [de Giberne]. John Betjeman and Dorset. Dorchester (Dorset): Dorset County Museum, May 1963. (Dorset Natural History and Archaeological Society Publications)

507. Sparrow, John. "The Poetry of John Betjeman," in Independent Essays by John Sparrow. London: Faber & Faber, 1963, p. 166-179.

508. _____, Preface to Selected Poems by John Betjeman. London: John Murray, 1952, p. ix-xxii.

509. Spender, Stephen. Poetry Since 1939. London: Longmans, 1946, p. 42.

510. Stanford, Derek. John Betjeman: A Study. London: Neville Spearman, 1961.
    For reviews see New Statesman, 61 (April 28, 1961), 672, 674, D. J. Enright; Observer, March 26, 1961, p. 31, Philip Toynbee; and Times Literary Supplement, 60, (April 14, 1961), 235.

511. Stern, Gladys Bronwyn. And Did He Stop and Speak to You? London: Coram, Published in

association with the Centaur Press, 1957; also
Chicago: Henry Regnery, 1958, p. 53-73.

512. Wain, John. "Four Observer Pieces: John
Betjeman," in Essays on Literature and Ideas,
by John Wain. London: Macmillan; New York:
St. Martin's Press, 1963, p. 168-171.

513. Who's Who, 1971-1972. New York: St. Martin's
Press, 1971, p. 259-260.

514. Wilson, Edmund. The Bit Between My Teeth: A
Literary Chronicle of 1950-1965. New York:
Farrar, Straus and Giroux, 1965, p. 385-386,
536.

515. Zeitgenössische englische Dichtung: Einführung
in die englische Literaturbetrachtung mit Interpre-
tationen. Frankfurt a. M. : Hirschgraben-Verlag,
1966. I. "Lyrik," by Horst Meller.
Includes "John Betjeman: Devonshire Street,
W. 1," by Hans-Joachim Zimmerman, p. 118-
125.

515a. Zimmerman, Hans-Joachim, "John Betjeman," in
Englische Dichter der Moderne: Ihr Leben und
Werk, by Rudolf Sühnel and Dieter Riesner. Ber-
lin: E. Schmidt, 1971, p. 510-519.

B. BIOGRAPHY AND CRITICISM: MAGAZINE ARTICLES

516. Allsop, Kenneth, "The Year of the Poet," <u>Daily Mail</u>, December 9. 1960, p. 8.

517. Barnes, Susan, " 'Betjeman, I Bet Your Racket Brings You in a Pretty Packet,' " <u>Sunday Times Magazine,</u> January 30, 1972, p. 8+.

518. Bergonzi, Bernard, "Culture and Mr. Betjeman: 'That's a Surrey Sunset,' " <u>20th Century,</u> 165 (February, 1959), 130-137 (May, 1959), 520.
    A review of the 1959 ed. of <u>John Betjeman's Collected Poems.</u> For a reply see "Culture and Mr. Betjeman," by Rosalind Constable, <u>20th Century,</u> 165 (April, 1959), 439.

519. Betjeman, Lady Penelope, "An Extremely Happy Life: Horses and Other Matters," <u>The Listener,</u> 88 (August 17, 1972), 193, 210-211.

520. "Betjemanism," the title of letters to the Editor in response to an article in <u>Spectator,</u> 198, (May 17, 1957), 645, by John Betjeman, one of the series, "Town and Country." See <u>Spectator,</u> 198 (May 31, 1957), 718; 198 (June 7, 1957), 750; 198 (June 14, 1957), 777; and 198 (June 21, 1957), 811-812.
    The subject is the reconstruction of the Albert Bridge.

521. Bishop, George W. "Poets, Critics and Wits," <u>Daily Telegraph,</u> September 26, 1957, p. 13.

522. Buchanan, Handasyde, "A Bookseller Surveys the

Past Year," Daily Telegraph, December 31, 1954, p. 8.

523. Carter, John, "Betjemaniana," Book Collector, 9 (Summer, 1960), 199 and 9 (Winter), 452.

524. Crookston, Peter, "Where Are They Now? Joan Hunter Dunn," Sunday Times Colour Supplement, August 8, 1965, p. 16-21.

525. Davie, Michael, "The Bard of the Railway Gas-Lamp," Observer, October 15, 1972, p. 9.

526. Devlin, Tim, "Sir John Betjeman, the New Poet Laureate: Summoned by Success," The Times (London), October 11, 1972, p. 16.

527. Driberg, Tom, "A Walk with Mr. Betjeman," New Statesman, 61 (January 6, 1961), 9-10.

528. Gardner, Raymond, "Sweetness and Light," Manchester Guardian, October 11, 1972, p. 10. (Daily ed.)

529. Gibson, Walker, "Speaking of Books," New York Times Book Review, January 31, 1960, p. 2.

530. Green, F. Pratt, "The New Poet Laureate: A Personal Appreciation," Expository Times, 84, January, 1973, p. 115-117.

531. Hern, Anthony, "The Princess's Poet: A John Betjeman Boutique," Daily Express, December 20, 1958, p. 4.

532. Hollander, John, "John Betjeman: Almost Uniquely Qualified," New York Times, October 11, 1972, p. 18.

533. Hollis, Christopher, "Best of Betjeman" [poem], Spectator, 205 (November 25, 1960), 819.

534. _____, "Mr. Betjeman As Thinker," The

Month, 207 (March, 1959), 166-170.

535. _____, "To Sir John" [poem], Spectator, 222 (June 28, 1969), 845.

536. Larkin, Philip, "The Blending of Betjeman," Spectator, 205 (December 2, 1960), 913.

536a. _____, "It Could Only Happen in England: A Study of John Betjeman's Poems for American Readers," Cornhill, No. 1069 (Autumn, 1971), 21-36.
Written as an introduction to the American edition of John Betjeman's Collected Poems.

537. Laurie, Peter, "Betjeman and Milligan on Melancholia," Sunday Times Magazine, March 19, 1967, p. 12.

538. "Major Minor Poet," Time, 73 (February 2, 1959), 70-71.

539. Mills, Ralph J., Jr., "John Betjeman's Poetry: An Appreciation," Descant, 13 (Spring, 1969), 2-18.

540. Moorhouse, Geoffrey, "Poet Communicant," Manchester Guardian, November 8, 1960, p. 7.

541. Neame, Alan, "Poet of Anglicanism," Commonweal, 71 (December 4, 1959), 282-284.

542. "New Poet Laureate," Newsweek, 80 (October 23, 1972), 60-65.

543. "The Observer Profile: John Betjeman," Observer February 8, 1959, p. 7.

544. Paulding, Gouverneur, "To Magdalen and Back," Reporter, 24 (February 16, 1961), 62-63.

545. "Pendennis," pseud., "Table Talk: Betjeman's Progress, Observer, August 13, 1961, p. 17.

546. "People," Time, 100 (October 23, 1972), 50.

547. Petschek, Willa, "The Betjeman Phenomenon,"
New York Times Magazine, August 13, 1967,
p. 24-25, 37, 39, 42, 44, 50, 52.

548. "Pharos," pseud., "A Spectator's Notebook,"
Spectator, 198 (April 5, 1957), 431-432.

549. Philpot, Terry, "Poet Floreat," Manchester
Guardian, June 19, 1970, p. 10.

550. Plomer, William, "At Home with Mr. Betjeman,"
Manchester Guardian, April 7, 1961, p. 7.

551. "Poet on Stopover," New Yorker, 33 (March 16,
1957), 22-24.

552. "Poet to the Sovereign: Sir John Betjeman," New
York Times, October 11, 1972, p. 18.

553. "Poetry and the Public," Times Literary Supplement, No. 2964, (December 19, 1958), 737.

554. "Poetry in Doubt," Times Literary Supplement
[44], (July 29, 1965), 649.

555. "Quoodle," pseud., "Spectator's Notebook,"
Spectator, 215 (August 13, 1965), 201-202.

556. "Result of Competition No. 878," New Statesman
and Nation, n. s. 33 (January 11, 1947), 36-37.
Seven poems imitating the Betjeman manner.
(January 18, 1947), 48. Betjeman contributes
a poem on the same subject, "Indoor Games
near Newbury."

557. "The Reticent Faith," "The British Imagination,"
Special Supplement, Times Literary Supplement,
September 9, 1960, p. iv.

558. Ross, Theodore J., "Life in Betjeman-land,"
New Republic, 141 (October 12, 1959), 18-19.

559. "Signs of an All Too Correct Compassion," "The
     British Imagination," Special Supplement, Times
     Literary Supplement, September 9, 1960, p. xiii.

560. Singh, Ghan S. "The Poetry of John Betjeman,"
     Studi e ricerche di letteratura: inglese e ameri-
     cana 1 (1967), 345-370.

561. "Sir John Betjeman: Poet Laureate in Ordinary,
     Who Felt Humbled," Times (London), October 11,
     1972, p. 1.

562. Spender, Stephen, "Poetry for Poetry's Sake and
     Poetry beyond Poetry," Horizon (London), 13
     (April, 1946), 221-238.

563. Stanford, Derek, "Ideology and Mr. Betjeman,"
     The Month, n. s. 24 (April, 1960), 240-246.

564. _____, "John Betjeman: Poet for Export?"
     Meanjin Quarterly, 20 (September, 1961), 315-
     319.

565. _____, "Mr. Betjeman's Satire," Contemporary
     Review, 197 (May 1960), 286-289.

566. _____, "The Poetry of John Betjeman, The
     Month, n. s. 19 (February, 1958), 84-88.

567. "Talk with the Author," Newsweek, 56 (Novem-
     ber 28, 1960), 89.

568. "Town Talk: 'By Appointment,' to Mrs. Wilson--
     John Betjeman," Sunday Express, May 5, 1968,
     p. 2.

569. Toynbee, Philip, "Poet of Time and Place,"
     Observer, December 7, 1958, p. 16.

570. _____, "Poet on the Plinth," Observer,
     March 26, 1961, p. 31.

571. Ullnaess, Sverre P. N., "John Betjeman:

Sjarmerende, betydelig engelsk dikter," Samtiden, 72 (October, 1963), 564-582.

572. Waugh, Auberon, "Royal Rhymster," New York Times Magazine, January 6, 1974, p. 18, 22, 24 and 26.

573. "Week-end Competitions," New Statesman and Nation, 33 (January 11, 1947), 36-37 and (January 18, 1947), 48.

574. Weightman, J. G., "The Culture Vulture: [Reading verse on the stage of the Lyceum]", 20th Century, 166 (October, 1959), 270-271.

575. Wiehe, R. E., "Summoned by Nostalgia: John Betjeman's Poetry," Arizona Quarterly, 19 (Spring, 1963), 37-49.

576. Young, Kenneth, "Poets Telling Tales," Daily Telegraph, October 4, 1957, p. 12.

577. _____, "Writers in the Wilderness," Daily Telegraph, June 6, 1955, p. 4.

C. REVIEWS OF JOHN BETJEMAN'S WORKS

Collected Poems

578. Alvarez, A., "London Letter: Exile's Return," Partisan Review, 26 (Spring, 1959), 284-289.

579. Bennett, Joseph, "Two Americans, a Brahmin, and the Bourgeoisie," Hudson Review, 12 (Autumn, 1959), 435-439.

580. Bevington, Helen, South Atlantic Quarterly, 59 (Winter, 1960), 125-127.

581. Bishop, Morris, "Witty and Nostalgic Verse," New York Herald Tribune Book Review, April 26, 1959, p. 5.

582. Bogan, Louise, "Verse," New Yorker, 35 (April 18, 1959), 169-170.

583. Buchan, Alastair, "Nostalgia for Steam Engines," Reporter, 20 (April 30, 1959), 39.

584. Buckle, Richard, "Topographical Laureate," Books and Bookmen, 18 (December, 1972), 11-13.

585. Choice, 9 (May, 1972), 366.

586. Dobbs, Kildare, "Auks in the Belfry," Tamarack Review No. 12, (Summer, 1959), 96-101.

587. Gibson, Walker, "Willing to See It All and Love It," New York Times Book Review, April 12, 1959, p. 6-7.

588. Gransden, K. W. The Listener, 60 (December 11, 1958), 1001, 1003.

589. Green, F. Pratt, "Worlds Apart," Poetry Review, 50 (April-June, 1959), 99-100.

590. Gunn, Thom, "Poets, English and American," Yale Review, n. s., 48 (June, 1959), 617-620.

591. Holmes, John, "Poetry Quarterly," Saturday Review, 42 (May 23, 1959), 42.

592. Kermode, Frank, "A Full Peal of Betjeman," Spectator, 201 (December 19, 1958), 896.

593. Larkin, Philip, "Betjeman en bloc," Listener, 3 (Spring, 1959), 14-22.

594. _____, "Poetry beyond a Joke," Manchester Guardian, December 19, 1958, p. 4.

595. "Major Minor Poet," Time, 73 (February 2, 1959), 70-71.

596. Mortimer, Raymond, "John Betjeman's Gentle Muse," The Sunday Times, November 30, 1958, p. 22.

597. Neame, Alan, "London Chronicle, I," Poetry, 94 (May, 1959), 124-127.

598. Plomer, William, London Magazine, 6 (March, 1959), 65-67.

599. Prescott, Orville, "Books of the Times," New York Times, April 13, 1959, p. 29, col. 3.

600. Pritchard, William H., Hudson Review, 25 (Spring, 1972), 130-132.

601. "Recollection," Times Literary Supplement, No. 3560 (May 21, 1970), 556.

602. Rosenthal, Macha Louis, "Tuning In on Albion,"
     Nation, 188 (May 16, 1959), 457-459.

603. Ross, T. J., "Life in Betjemanland," New
     Republic, 141 (October 12, 1959), 18-19.

604. "A Serious Poet," Times Literary Supplement,
     No. 2963 (December 12, 1958), 720.
     Followed by correspondence, "Meade Falkner
     and Mr. Betjeman," by Geoffrey Grigson
     (December 19, 1958), 737 and by reply by the
     reviewer [John Sparrow] (January 2, 1959), 7.

605. Smith, Janet Adam, "--And Betjeman's Verses,"
     New Statesman, 56 (December 6, 1958), 819-820.

606. Stork, Charles Wharton, "John Betjeman's Col-
     lected Poems," Wings (Mill Valley, Calif.)
     (Winter, 1960), 25.

607. Thompson, J. W. M., "Forty Years On,"
     Spectator, 224 (April 18, 1970), 515-516.

                    Altar and Pew

608. Clark, Leonard, Time and Tide, 41 (February 13,
     1960), 173.

        Collins Guide to English Parish Churches
    (American edition has title An American's Guide ...)

609. E., R., Connoisseur (American edition), 143
     (April, 1959), 112.

610. Hutton, Graham, "Parochiale Anglicanum,"
     Spectator, 201 (December 5, 1958), 832.

611. Landgren, Marchal E., Library Journal, 84
     (March 1, 1959), 736.

612. Metcalf, Priscilla, Royal Institute of British Architects Journal, Series 3, 66 (March, 1959), 179.

613. Nairn, Ian, "Intermittent Enthusiasm," Architectural Review, 128 (November, 1960), 323.

614. Rowntree, Diana, Manchester Guardian, November 25, 1958, p. 4.

615. "Signposts to the Parish Church," Times Literary Supplement, No. 2958 (November 7, 1958), 645.

616. Wakin, Jeanette, "Travelers Tales," Saturday Review, 42 (March 14, 1959), 52.

617. Wordsworth, Andrew, "Betjeman's Churches," New Statesman, 56 (December 6, 1958), 818-819.

Collins Pocket Guide to English Parish Churches

617a. Killick, John. "Betjeman's Churches," Architectural Review, 145 (January, 1969), 71.

618. Meath, Gerard, O. P. "The Parish Church," Tablet, 222 (July 20, 1968), 720-721.

619. Middleton, Robin, "Getting About," Architectural Design, 42 (February, 1972), 118.

620. Spectator, 221 (July 12, 1968), 61.

Continual Dew

621. Quennell, Peter, "Flowers of Mediocrity," New Statesman and Nation, n. s. 14 (November 13, 1937), 802, 804.

Cornwall

622. Jones, D. A. N. , "Poetic Justice," New States-
     man, n.s. 67 (June 19, 1964), 961-962.

623. Rowse, A. L. , "Across the Tamar," Spectator,
     213 (July 10, 1964), 52.

624. "Tin or Trippers," Times Literary Supplement,
     [63] (September 17, 1964), 862.

English Churches

625. P. , J. C. , "English Churches," R. I. B. A.
     Journal, ser. 3, 72 (March, 1965), 147.

626. Times Literary Supplement, No. 3245 (May 7,
     1964), 388.

English Cities and Small Towns

627. Anderson, M. D. , "English Cities and Small
     Towns," Architectural Review, 93 (May 1943),
     136.

628. "English Towns," Times Literary Supplement,
     [42] (February 27, 1943), 106.

629. The Listener, 29 (June 3, 1943), 670.

630. Postbridge, Warren, "Britain in Pictures,"
     Spectator, 170 (March 12, 1943), 250.

English Love Poems

631. Graham, Stephen, "The Food of Love," Poetry

Review, 49 (April-June, 1958), 102-103.

632. Gransden, K. W., The Listener, 58 (December 5, 1957), 939.

633. Sergeant, Howard, "Poetry Review," English 12 (Spring, 1958), 26-28.

634. "The Tree of Love," Times Literary Supplement, [56] (November 15, 1957), 691.

English, Scottish and Welsh Landscape

635. "British Landscape," Times Literary Supplement, [43] (August 26, 1944), 409.

636. The Listener, 32 (August 24, 1944), 217.

A Few Late Chrysanthemums

637. Arlott, John, "Fashion and Passion," Spectator, 193 (July 16, 1954), 98.

638. Betjeman, John, "John Betjeman Replies," Spectator, 193 (October 8, 1954), 441.

639. Fraser, G. S., "Texture and Structure," New Statesman and Nation, 48 (July 31, 1954), 127-138.

640. The Listener, 52 (August 5, 1954), 221.

641. Taylor, Geoffrey, Time and Tide, 35 (July 17, 1954), 971.

First and Last Loves

642. Casson, Hugh, Royal Institute of British

Architects Journal, ser, 3, 60 (April, 1953),
247-248.

643. Lancaster, Osbert, "The Unfashionable Past,"
The Listener, 48 (October 9, 1952), 605, 607.

644. Summerson, John, "In the Betjeman Country,"
New Statesman and Nation, 44 (October 4, 1952),
382.

645. Times Literary Supplement, [51] (October 24,
1952), 685-686.

Ghastly Good Taste

646. "Betjeman in the Beginning," T. L. S.: The
Times Literary Supplement, No. 3599,
(February 19, 1971), 216.

647. Burdett, Osbert, "Belles Lettres," London Mercury, 28 (September, 1933), 466-468.

648. _____, "Christendom to Capital," Architectural
Review, 74 (October, 1933), 142.

649. Choice, 9 (October, 1972), 958.

650. Goodhart-Rendel, H. S., "The Critic and the
Builder," Spectator, 151 (August 11, 1933), 197.

651. Mullin, Stephen, "Fandango," New Statesman, 80
(December 18, 1970), 844.

652. R., P., Connoisseur, 92 (November, 1933), 334.

653. White, Terence de Vere, "The Gospel According
to John," Spectator, 225 (November 14, 1970),
602.

High and Low

654. Bewley, Maurice, "Good Manners," New York
Review of Books, 8 (May 18, 1967), 31-34.

655. Blunden, Edmund, "Poetry, Light and Dark,"
Daily Telegraph, November 10, 1966, p. 20.

656. "Branch Line," Times Literary Supplement, [65]
(November 10, 1966), 1021.

657. Carey, John, "Unpolitical Auden," New Statesman,
72 (December 23, 1966), 941-942.

658. Cayton, Robert F., "Poetry," Library Journal,
92 (July, 1967), 2582.

659. Choice, 4 (December, 1967), 1114.

660. Church, Richard, "Beware of the Laughter!"
Poetry Review, 58 (Summer, 1967), 154-157.

661. Cox, C. B., "Betjemanland," Spectator, 217
(December 9, 1966), 763.

662. Curtis, Anthony, "Mellow Voices," Sunday Telegraph, November 6, 1966, p. 17.

663. Gross, John, "Betjemanesque," The Observer,
November 6, 1966, p. 26.

664. Harriott, John F. X., S.J. "Home Counties,"
The Month, 37 (January, 1967), 62-63.

665. McCord, David, "A Special Taste," New York
Times Book Review, September 24, 1967, p. 57.

666. Martin, Graham, "New Poetry," The Listener,
77 (January 26, 1967), 140.

667. Meath, Gerard, O.P., "To Dissolution Nearer
Now," Tablet, 220 (December 24, 1966), 1447.

120   Sir John Betjeman

668. Press, John, "Change and Decay," Punch, 251
     (November 23, 1966), 789.

669. Ross, Alan, "Poetry," London Magazine n.s. 6
     (March 1967), 94-96.

670. Russell, Arthur, "Book Talk: High and Low,"
     BBC European Services, General News Talk,
     November 3, 1966. Unpublished.

671. Turco, Lewis, "Of Laureates and Lovers,"
     Saturday Review, 50 (October 14, 1967), 99.

672. Varyl, Richard, Books & Bookmen, 12 (May,
     1967), 27.

673. "Verse," New Yorker, 43 (September 2, 1967),
     87-88.

                    A Hundred Sonnets

674. "Old Ruralities," Times Literary Supplement,
     No. 3069 (December 23, 1960), 830.

675. Wood, Frederick T., "Current Literature, 1960,"
     English Studies [Amsterdam], (August, 1961), 267.

                    John Piper

676. Baxandall, D. K., "John Piper," Museums
     Journal, 45 (October, 1945), 124-125.

677. Hoffmann, Edith, Burlington Magazine, 88
     (January, 1946), 25.

678. "Painting Contrasts," Times Literary Supplement,
     [44] (February 17, 1945), 82.

679. Wallis, N. A. D., "Notes on Books," Royal

Society of Arts Journal, 94 (January 18, 1946), 130.

London's Historic Railway Stations

680. Annan, Gabriel, "Sir John and the Dragon," The Listener, 88 (July 6, 1972), 22.

681. Dougill, David, "Betjeman's Railway Stations," Books and Bookmen, 17 (August, 1972), 53-54.

682. History Today, 22 (July, 1972), 527.

683. "London Pride," Economist, 243 (June 24, 1972), 63.

684. "London's Termini, Is It the End?" Times Literary Supplement, No. 3680 (September 15, 1972), 1050.

685. Nuttgens, Patrick, "Cathedrals of Steam," Design (London) No. 284 (August, 1972), 72.

Mount Zion

686. Churchill, Randolph, "Arts and Crafts," Architectural Review, 70 (December, 1931), 184.

687. "Looking Backward," Times Literary Supplement, November 26, 1931, p. 944.

688. Pryce-Jones, Alan, "Chronicles: Poetry," London Mercury, 25 (December, 1931), 202-203.

Murray's Berkshire Architectural Guide

689. Gardiner, Stephen, Royal Institute of British

Architects Journal, ser. 3, 57 (November, 1949), 28.

690. K. , H. Werk, 37, supplement (September, 1950), 132.

691. Tunnard, Christopher, "Unmodern County," Architectural Review, 106 (December, 1949), 401.

Murray's Buckinghamshire Architectural Guide

692. Fedden, Robin, "The Turn of the Tide?" Architectural Review, 105 (April, 1949), 198.

693. K. , H. Werk, 37, supplement (September, 1950), 132.

694. "Traveller's Joy," Times Literary Supplement, [47] (August 21, 1948), 472.

695. Yerbury, F. R. , Royal Institute of British Architects Journal, ser. 3, 56 (April, 1949), 286.

New Bats in Old Belfries

696. Casson, Hugh, "Betjeman in the Belfry," Architectural Review, 100 (July, 1946), 29-30.

697. The Listener, 35 (February 14, 1946), 217.

698. "Mr. Betjeman's Work," Times Literary Supplement, [45] (January 5, 1946), 8.

699. Rees, Goronwy, "Clever and Good," Spectator, 176 (February 15, 1946), 176.

Old Lights for New Chancels

700. The Listener, 23 (January-June, 1940), Supplement 49, vii.

701. Rees, Goronwy, "An Original Poet," Spectator, 164 (May 3, 1940), 636, 638.

702. "Senex," pseud., "Neo-Romantic," New Statesman and Nation, n. s. 19 (March 30, 1940), 439-440.

703. "Some Modern Poets," Times Literary Supplement, [40] (March 23, 1940), 148.

An Oxford University Chest

704. Greene, Graham, "Oxford Infelix," Spectator, 161 (December 16, 1938), 1053.

705. Hastings, Maurice, Architectural Review, 85 (May, 1939), 257-259.

706. The Listener, 20 (December 29, 1938), 1424.

707. "Miscellaneous," London Mercury, 39 (February, 1939), 474.

A Pictorial History of English Architecture

708. Buckle, Richard, "Betjeman on English Architecture," Books and Bookmen, 18 (October, 1972), 22-23.

709. "London's Termini, Is It the End?" Times Literary Supplement, No. 3680 (September 15, 1972), 1050.

710. New Yorker, 48 (December 9, 1972), 178-179.

711. "Under $15.00," Time, 100 (December 4, 1972), 74.

712. World, 1 (December 19, 1972), 64.

A Ring of Bells

713. "Fine Excess: Verse for All Tastes," Times Literary Supplement, No. 3169 (November 23, 1962), 893.

714. Jackson, Katherine Gauss, "Books in Brief," Harper's Magazine, 227 (July, 1963), 94.

715. Larkin, Philip, "Open Your Betjemans," Spectator, 209 (November 9, 1962), 726.

716. Levy, William Turner, "For Younger Readers," New York Times Book Review, August 4, 1963, p. 24-25.

717. Libby, Margaret Sherwood, "How to Kiss a Princess," Book Week, 1 (October 27, 1963), 20.

718. "Riding a Centaur," Newsweek, 56 (November 28, 1960), 89.

719. Rudin, Ellen, Library Journal, 88 (July, 1963), 2779-2780.

Selected Poems

720. Craig, H. A. L., "Poetry," Spectator, 181 (December 10, 1948), 774, 776.

721. "The Listener's Book Chronicle," The Listener, 41 (February 3, 1949), 196.

722. "Slopes of Mount Zion," Times Literary

Supplement, [47] (October 9, 1948), 567.

723. Wordsworth, Andrew, "Selected Betjeman," New Statesman and Nation, 36 (December 11, 1948), 532-533.

Shell Guide to Cornwall

724. H., A. W., "A New Sort of Guidebook," Architectural Review, 76 (August, 1934), 60-61.

Shropshire

725. "County Guide," Times Literary Supplement, [50] (December 21, 1951), 818.

726. The Listener, 46 (November 29, 1951), 938.

727. Spectator, 187 (November 2, 1951), 584.

Slick But Not Streamlined

728. Bogan, Louise, "Verse," New Yorker, 23 (September 13, 1947), 118.

729. Edman, Irwin, "Tender Satire on English Ways," New York Herald Tribune Weekly Book Review, 24 (September 14, 1947), 6.

730. Frye, Northrop, "The Betjeman Brand," Poetry, 71 (December, 1947), 162-165. Reprinted in Poetry, 121 (October, 1972), 48-50.

731. Humphries, Rolfe, "John Betjeman," Nation, 165 (September 27, 1947), 316.

732. Lyons, Herbert, "A Special Englishman," New

York Times Book Review, August 24, 1947, p. 7
and 25.

733. McLaughlin, Richard, "English Topophil,"
Saturday Review of Literature, 30 (August 16,
1947), 29.

734. "Small Wreath," Time, 50 (July 28, 1947), 90-91.

735. Watts, Richard, "The Real Thing," New Republic,
117 (August 4, 1947), 28-29.

Summoned by Bells

736. Allen, Walter, "A Georgian Boyhood," New York
Times Book Review, November 27, 1960, p. 5
and 30.

737. Broadbent, John, "Highgate Bore Me," Time and
Tide, 41 (December 3, 1960), 1486.

738. Christian Century, 78 (February 22, 1961), 249.

739. Cogswell, Fred, "Summoned by Bells," Canadian
Forum, 40 (March, 1961), 286.

740. Derrick, Christopher, "The Prelude," Tablet,
214 (December 3, 1960), 1118, 1120.

741. Furbank, P. N., "O Mappin, Webb, Asprey and
Finnigan," The Listener, 64 (December 1, 1960),
999.

742. Gibson, Walker, "Summoned by Betjeman,"
Poetry, 97 (March, 1961), 390-391.

743. Graham, Stephen, "The Schooldays of John Betjeman," Poetry Review, 52 (April-June, 1961), 98.

744. Highet, Gilbert, "Summoned by Bells," Book-of-
the-Month Club News, December, 1960, p. 10-11.

745. Irwin, Joan, Tamarack Review, 18 (Winter, 1961), 90-91.

746. Kermode, Frank, "Henry Miller and John Betjeman," Encounter, 16 (March, 1961), 69-75.

747. "Knowing Mr. Betjeman," Times Literary Supplement, No. 3066 (December 2, 1960), 776.

748. Kunitz, Stanley, Harper's Magazine, 223 (August, 1961), 88.

749. Larkin, Philip, "The Blending of Betjeman," Spectator, 205 (December 2, 1960), 913.

750. Macbeth, George, London Magazine, 8 (February, 1961), 76-79.

751. Morse, Samuel French, "Seven Poets, Present Tense," Virginia Quarterly Review, 37 (Spring, 1961), 291-293.

752. Paulding, Gouverneur, "To Magdalen and Back," Reporter, 24 (February 16, 1961), 62-63.

753. Plomer, William, "Poet Face to Face," Daily Telegraph, December 2, 1960, 18.

754. Prescott, Orville, "Books of the Times," New York Times, November 28, 1960, p. 29.

755. Pritchett, V. S., "Betjeman in Pooterland," New Statesman, 60 (December 3, 1960), 894.

756. Pryce-Jones, Alan, "Autobiography in Blank Verse," New York Herald Tribune Lively Arts, 37 (December 4, 1960), 32.

757. Richart, Bette, "Few Facts, Many Values," Commonweal, 73 (March 3, 1961), 592-594.

758. Robie, Burton A., Library Journal, 86 (February 15, 1961), 802.

759. Simpson, Louis, "Important and Unimportant Poems," Hudson Review, 14 (Autumn, 1961), 469.

760. Symons, Julian, "Private Giggles," Punch, 239 (December 28, 1960), 951.

761. "To Be a Poet," Time, 76 (December 5, 1960), 92.

762. Wood, Frederick T., "Current Literature, 1960," English Studies (Amsterdam), 42 (August, 1961), 265-266.

Victorian and Edwardian Brighton

763. "Local History," Times Literary Supplement, No. 3669 (June 23, 1972), 730.

Victorian and Edwardian London

764. Hale, William Harlan, "History for Christmas," New York Times Book Review, December 7, 1969, p. 44.

765. New Yorker, 46 (May 23, 1970), 140.

766. Pritchett, V. S., "Fog and Corsets," New States-man, 78 (October 3, 1969), 463-464.

767. Stafford, Jean, Book World, September 27, 1970, p. 6.

768. "Travel and Topography," Times Literary Supplement, No. 3535 (November 27, 1969), 1370.

769. Turley, G. E., "History," Library Journal, 95 (February 1, 1970), 492.

Victorian and Edwardian Oxford

770. Annan, Gabriel, "Fading and Gone," The Listener, 87 (January 6, 1972), 24.

771. "Evocations in Sepia," Times Literary Supplement, No. 3646 (January 14, 1972), 43.

INDEX OF POEMS

131

134   Sir John Betjeman

Group Life: Letchworth 1-4, 6, 7, 18, 20-22, 28

Hail! poet artist of the age of steam:/ 122
Harrow-on-the-Hill 1-4, 6, 7, 9, 14, 20-22, 146,
    466, 467
Harvest Hymn 6, 7, 11-13, 191
The Heart of Thomas Hardy 1-4, 6, 7, 466, 467
Henley-on-Thames 1-4, 6, 7, 14, 16, 17, 20-25,
    236, 466
Hertfordshire 1-4, 6, 7, 20-22, 184
A Hike on the Downs 1-4, 6-8
Holy Trinity, Sloane Street MCMVII 1-4, 6, 7, 18
The Hon. Sec. 6, 7, 11-13
House of Rest 1-4, 6, 7, 9, 14, 466
How to Get On in Society 1-4, 6, 7, 9, 14, 20-22,
    27, 98, 99, 187, 237
Hundreds of birds in the air/ 238, 239
Hunter Trials 1-4, 6, 7, 9, 14, 20-22, 146, 156,
    173, 240, 466
Huxley Hall 1-4, 6, 7, 9
Hymn 1-4, 6-8, 14, 15, 20-25

I. M. Walter Ramsden, ob. March 26, 1947, Pembroke
    College, Oxford 1-4, 6, 7, 175, 466, 467 (For
    variant title see item 9)
An Impoverished Irish Peer 1-4, 6-8, 28
In a Bath Teashop 1-4, 6, 7, 16, 17, 23-25, 28, 73,
    74, 139, 149, 466, 467
In Memoriam: A. C., R. J. O., K. S. 183, 241,
    242
In Memory of Basil, Marquess of Dufferin and Ava
    1-4, 6, 7, 16, 17, 28
In the Public Gardens 1-4, 6, 7, 20-22, 183, 243,
    244, 467
In Westminster Abbey 1-4, 6, 7, 18, 27, 28, 137,
    140, 141, 144, 157, 166, 169-171, 193, 195, 197,
    471
In Willesden Churchyard 6, 11-13, 245
An Incident in the Early Life of Ebenezer Jones, Poet,
    1828 1-4, 6, 7, 18, 20-25, 144
Indoor Games near Newbury 1-4, 6, 7, 20-25, 179,
    180, 246, 556

NAME INDEX